THE HABITS AND TRAITS OF A MILLIONAIRE

Understanding the Millionaire Mindset

Dr. Maxwell Shimba

Shimba Publishing, LLC.

Printed by Shimba Publishing LLC
Printed in the United States of America

TABLE OF CONTENTS

INTRODUCTION

The Habits and Traits of a Millionaire

Understanding the Millionaire Mindset

In today's world, financial success is often viewed as a hallmark of personal achievement and influence. Millionaires represent a unique class of individuals who have attained significant wealth through diverse means—whether through entrepreneurship, investments, innovation, or even inheritance. However, what truly distinguishes millionaires is not merely the accumulation of wealth but the distinctive habits, traits, and mindset that lead to such financial prosperity.

What makes millionaires stand out? Is it their ability to take risks, their discipline in managing resources, or their relentless pursuit of growth? These questions form the foundation of this book. The millionaire mindset is not a mystery; rather, it is a series of principles and habits that, when applied consistently, can yield remarkable results.

The purpose of this book is to delve deep into the habits, strategies, and characteristics that define millionaires. Whether you are starting your journey toward financial freedom or seeking to refine your existing approach, understanding these patterns will provide valuable insights into how you can cultivate the mindset required for long-term success.

Throughout this book, we will explore key themes such as goal setting, discipline, risk-taking, learning, resilience, financial literacy, and the importance of relationships. These themes not only form the foundation of a millionaire's life but also offer practical strategies that can be implemented by anyone seeking to elevate their financial standing.

The goal is to move beyond mere admiration of millionaires and their lifestyles. Instead, the focus will be on understanding the blueprint of their success—what they do, how they think, and why they consistently achieve high levels of prosperity.

Understanding the millionaire mindset goes beyond acquiring financial knowledge. It requires an evolution of thought, discipline, and focus. Whether your aspirations are modest or grand, the principles discussed in this book will serve as a guide to achieving lasting financial success and personal fulfillment.

As we embark on this journey, keep in mind that the millionaire mindset is accessible to anyone willing to adopt the right habits and consistently apply them. It's not about luck or being in the right place at the right time; it's about making conscious, intentional decisions that align with your financial goals and values.

Let's get started on this path of discovery, and in the following chapters, uncover the habits and traits that can lead to your own financial success.

DR. MAXWELL SHIMBA

CHAPTER 01

THE POWER OF VISION AND GOAL SETTING

One of the most defining traits of millionaires is their ability to think long-term. While others may focus on immediate gains or short-term gratification, millionaires operate with a clear vision of where they want to be in the future. This long-term thinking is not just a vague dream or hope but is grounded in concrete goals and actionable steps. The power of vision and goal setting lies at the heart of their financial success.

The Importance of Vision

Vision is the foundation of any great achievement. It provides direction, purpose, and clarity. Without a clear vision, it's easy to get lost in day-to-day distractions and lose focus on what truly matters. Millionaires have a strong sense of where they are headed, often visualizing their future success with vivid detail. This vision acts as a compass, guiding their decisions and actions.

A powerful vision answers fundamental questions like:

- Where do I want to be financially in 5, 10, or 20 years?

- What kind of lifestyle do I want to live?

- What legacy do I want to leave behind?

Millionaires often think in terms of legacy and long-term impact. Their vision is not just about accumulating wealth but about creating lasting value for themselves, their families, and often, their communities.

Setting SMART Goals

To translate vision into reality, millionaires set specific, measurable, attainable, relevant, and time-bound (SMART) goals. These goals provide a roadmap for turning their vision into actionable steps. Let's break down the SMART criteria:

1. Specific: Millionaires are clear about what they want to achieve. Instead of vague goals like "I want to be rich," they set specific targets such as "I want to save $1 million for retirement by age 50."

2. Measurable: It's essential to track progress. Millionaires use measurable metrics to gauge success. For example, if their goal is to increase their net worth, they track the exact dollar amount they need to reach at certain intervals.

3. Attainable: While millionaires set ambitious goals, they ensure their goals are realistic and achievable. They push themselves to reach new heights without setting themselves up for failure.

4. Relevant: Every goal aligns with their overall vision. Millionaires do not waste time on activities or goals that do not contribute to their long-term financial objectives. Relevance keeps them focused and prevents distractions.

5. Time-bound: Every goal has a deadline. Millionaires understand the importance of setting timeframes to create a sense of urgency and momentum. For example, "I will increase my passive income by $50,000 within two years."

By setting SMART goals, millionaires break down their long-term vision into manageable, actionable steps, making it easier to achieve significant financial milestones.

The Role of a Vision Board

A vision board is a powerful tool that many millionaires use to keep their goals and dreams front and center. By visually representing their goals—whether through pictures, quotes, or symbols—millionaires create a constant reminder of what they are working toward. This serves as both inspiration and motivation.

A vision board can include:

- Images of dream homes, cars, or vacations

- Inspirational quotes related to success and financial freedom

- Pictures representing family, philanthropy, or career milestones

Seeing these visual cues daily helps keep their goals top of mind and reinforces their commitment to achieving them.

Maintaining a Success Journal

Alongside a vision board, many millionaires maintain a success journal. This journal serves as a personal record of their progress, challenges, and achievements. By regularly documenting their journey, millionaires can reflect on what's working, what needs adjustment, and how far they've come.

A success journal can include:

- Daily, weekly, or monthly goals

- Reflections on what was achieved and what could be improved

- Insights gained from books, seminars, or mentors

- Strategies for overcoming obstacles

The practice of journaling fosters self-awareness and accountability. It helps millionaires stay focused on their long-term goals while celebrating short-term wins along the way.

Reviewing and Adjusting Goals

One critical aspect of goal setting that sets millionaires apart is their flexibility and willingness to review and adjust goals as necessary. They understand that circumstances can change, and being adaptable is essential for continued growth.

Successful individuals frequently review their goals to ensure they remain aligned with their vision. If a particular strategy isn't yielding the desired results, they're not afraid to pivot or reassess their approach. Adjusting goals doesn't mean giving up; rather, it's about being strategic and making the necessary changes to stay on course.

Examples of Millionaires with Powerful Visions

1. Elon Musk: Musk's vision for space exploration and renewable energy has shaped his ambitious goals. His companies, Tesla and SpaceX, are direct results of his long-term vision to revolutionize transportation on Earth and beyond.

2. Oprah Winfrey: Oprah's success is deeply rooted in her vision of creating a media empire that empowers and inspires people. Her journey from humble beginnings to media mogul is a testament to her ability to set clear, impactful goals aligned with her vision.

3. Warren Buffet: Known as one of the most successful investors of all time, Buffett's long-term vision has been to create wealth through smart, patient investing. His disciplined approach to goal setting and adherence to his vision of value investing has paid off tremendously.

Building Your Vision and Goals

To adopt the habits of a millionaire, it's essential to start with a clear vision and effective goal-setting strategies. By establishing a strong sense of purpose, breaking it down into actionable steps, and regularly reviewing progress, you can create a roadmap for financial success. Whether you use tools like a vision board or a success journal, or simply practice regular self-reflection, the key is to stay focused, committed, and adaptable.

Verifiable examples of the power of vision and goal setting are found in many stories of self-made millionaires and entrepreneurs who used this principle to achieve extraordinary success. One notable example is Elon Musk, the visionary entrepreneur behind companies like Tesla, SpaceX, and SolarCity. Musk's success is rooted in his ability to set audacious goals with long-term vision, such as his mission to make space exploration affordable and to ultimately colonize Mars. When he founded SpaceX in 2002, his goal was not only to develop a viable space exploration company but also to make human life multi-planetary—a vision that has driven him through multiple setbacks, including early rocket failures and financial struggles. Despite these challenges, Musk's persistence and focus on his long-term vision helped SpaceX become the first private company to send humans to the International Space Station in 2020.

Another example of the power of vision and goal setting is Oprah Winfrey, who rose from poverty to become one of the wealthiest and most influential women in the world. Oprah's journey is a testament to how a clear vision, coupled with consistent goal setting, can lead to massive success. Early in her career, she set her sights on creating a media empire that would empower and inspire people. Her goal wasn't just to achieve personal fame but to provide a platform for transformative conversations. By setting clear, measurable goals along the way, Oprah expanded her brand beyond television, launching her own production company, Oprah Winfrey Network (OWN), and investing in various philanthropic efforts. Her disciplined pursuit of her goals, grounded in her long-term vision, has made her a billionaire and a global icon.

Lastly, Warren Buffett, one of the world's most successful investors, offers another prime example of the power of goal setting. Buffett began setting goals for his financial future at an early age. By age 11, he had already purchased his first stock and by 15, he was running a successful pinball machine business. Buffett's vision was clear from the start: to build lasting wealth through smart, disciplined investing. Throughout his career, he set specific financial goals for his investment firm, Berkshire Hathaway, and maintained a long-term perspective on wealth-building. By staying focused on his vision and making calculated decisions based on well-defined goals, Buffett transformed Berkshire Hathaway into one of the most valuable companies in the world and solidified his own status as a billionaire.

These examples underscore how setting a clear vision and establishing actionable goals are not just theoretical concepts but proven strategies employed by some of the world's most successful individuals. Their ability to think long-term, create measurable goals, and stay focused through challenges provides a roadmap for anyone aiming to achieve similar success.

To adapt the habit of vision and goal setting as described in this Chapter, an individual must follow several actionable steps that align with the practices of successful millionaires. Here's a breakdown of what someone can do:

1. Develop a Clear Vision

The first step is to create a clear and compelling long-term vision for your life or business. Think about where you want to be in the next 5, 10, or 20 years. Your vision should be something that excites and motivates you, but it must also be realistic enough to pursue. Take time to reflect on your passions, strengths, and the kind of impact you want to make in the world. Writing down your vision and visualizing your future success daily helps make it more tangible. For example, like Elon Musk, think beyond the immediate future and focus on big, transformative goals.

Practical Tip: Create a vision board by collecting images, quotes, or symbols that represent your ultimate goals. Place it somewhere you can see it daily to keep your focus on the big picture.

2. Set SMART Goals

After defining your vision, break it down into specific, measurable, attainable, relevant, and time-bound (SMART) goals. These goals are the stepping stones that will help you turn your vision into reality. Focus on both short-term and long-term goals, ensuring that each smaller goal aligns with your larger vision. For instance, if you aim to start a business, your goals might include researching the market, saving a certain amount of money, or gaining relevant skills. These concrete goals provide a roadmap, making progress measurable and motivating.

Practical Tip: Break your vision into yearly, quarterly, and monthly goals. Use tools like journals, planners, or goal-setting apps to track your progress.

3. Review and Adjust Regularly

Successful individuals like Oprah Winfrey and Warren Buffett consistently review and adjust their goals based on their progress and changing circumstances. To develop this habit, schedule regular check-ins with yourself, whether weekly, monthly, or quarterly, to evaluate how far you've come and make necessary adjustments. Life and business are unpredictable, so being adaptable is key to ensuring your goals remain relevant and attainable as you move forward.

Practical Tip: Keep a "success journal" where you document your progress, challenges, and lessons learned. This habit will keep you accountable, provide clarity, and allow you to reflect on your journey.

By following these steps and committing to the practice of vision and goal setting, individuals can adopt a habit that not only helps them stay focused on their dreams but also ensures consistent progress toward success.

CHAPTER 02

DISCIPLINE AND CONSISTENCY

If there is one trait that distinguishes millionaires from the average person, it is discipline. While motivation may come and go, discipline is what keeps millionaires moving forward when the excitement of the journey fades or when obstacles arise. Discipline, coupled with consistency, forms the backbone of their success.

The truth is, achieving long-term financial success requires more than just setting goals. It requires the disciplined follow-through of habits, routines, and actions that, over time, build toward significant results. In this chapter, we will explore how discipline and consistency play critical roles in maintaining focus on long-term goals, and how millionaires build daily routines that propel them forward, no matter the circumstances.

The Power of Daily Routines

One of the hallmarks of a millionaire's success is the structure of their daily routine. Millionaires are deliberate with their time, understanding that how they manage their day dictates their future outcomes. While the specifics of routines may vary from person to person, the underlying principle remains the same: consistency in action leads to success.

Daily routines help millionaires stay focused, productive, and on track with their goals. Rather than relying on bursts of motivation, they build habits that support their long-term vision. These habits often include:

- Morning Rituals: Many millionaires start their day early, using the quiet morning hours to focus on personal growth, planning, and setting the tone for a productive day. This time is often spent exercising, meditating, reading, or reviewing goals. Successful people understand that the way they start their day has a direct impact on how they perform throughout it.

- Prioritizing the Most Important Tasks: Discipline means knowing which tasks will bring the most value to achieving long-term goals. Millionaires follow the principle of "eating the frog," or tackling the hardest, most important task first. This ensures that critical objectives are met before distractions or lower-priority items take over the day.

- Time Blocking: To maintain consistency in action, millionaires often use time-blocking methods. They schedule specific blocks of time for focused work, meetings, self-development, and even rest. This structured approach prevents wasted time and keeps their day aligned with their goals.

- Evening Reflection: Before winding down, many millionaires take time to review their day, reflecting on what they achieved, what could have gone better, and how they can improve tomorrow. This nightly reflection reinforces self-discipline by fostering self-awareness and accountability.

Time Management and Focus

Time is the one resource that everyone has in equal measure, yet it's how millionaires manage their time that sets them apart. They understand that time is money, and the way they allocate their time determines their level of success. For them, effective time management is not just about doing more things, but about doing the right things.

Here's how millionaires manage their time to maintain discipline and consistency:

- The 80/20 Rule (Pareto Principle): Millionaires know that 80% of their success comes from 20% of their activities. By identifying which tasks have the highest impact on their financial goals, they can focus their energy where it truly counts. This allows them to work smarter, not harder, ensuring that their time is spent on high-value activities.

- Minimizing Distractions: Millionaires are masters of focus. They create environments that minimize distractions, whether that means turning off notifications, limiting social media, or scheduling focused work sessions without interruptions. By guarding their focus, they protect their time and ensure that each hour is used productively.

- Delegation: Understanding that they cannot do everything themselves, millionaires are skilled at delegating tasks that don't require their direct attention. Whether hiring assistants, outsourcing work, or automating processes, they free up time to concentrate on their areas of strength and high-value activities.

- Batching Tasks: To maximize efficiency, many successful individuals "batch" similar tasks together. For example, they may allocate specific times for emails, calls, or administrative tasks, completing them all in one focused session. This minimizes the mental energy wasted in constantly switching between different types of tasks.

Discipline as the Key to Long-Term Success

Discipline is what separates those who set goals from those who achieve them. For millionaires, discipline is not just about working hard; it's about working consistently over time, even when the results are not immediately visible. Discipline requires patience, perseverance, and the ability to delay gratification for the sake of a larger goal.

Here's how discipline shows up in a millionaire's life:

- Sticking to Financial Plans: Millionaires follow strict financial plans that align with their long-term goals. This means budgeting, saving, and investing consistently, even when temptations arise to spend impulsively. Whether it's avoiding luxury purchases or sticking to an investment strategy, disciplined financial habits help them grow their wealth over time.

- Sacrificing Short-Term Pleasure: Discipline often means sacrificing short-term pleasures for long-term rewards. Millionaires are willing to forgo immediate gratification— whether it's avoiding unnecessary purchases or working late to complete a project—because they understand the value of compounding effort over time.

- Pushing Through Setbacks: Discipline is what keeps millionaires moving forward when challenges arise. While others may give up in the face of difficulty, millionaires rely on their self-discipline to push through obstacles. Whether it's a failed business venture, a poor investment, or a market downturn, they remain committed to their goals.

- Building Positive Habits: Discipline is the force behind the consistent practice of habits that contribute to success. From waking up early, to exercising regularly, to continually learning and growing, millionaires practice the discipline of habit-building, knowing that small, consistent actions lead to substantial results.

Consistency Over Time

Consistency is the multiplier of discipline. While discipline gets you started, consistency is what carries you through to the finish line. Millionaires understand that success is not about grand, one-time efforts, but about steady, repeated actions over months and years.

Here's why consistency is crucial:

- The Compound Effect: Small, consistent actions accumulate over time to create massive results. Just as compound interest grows wealth exponentially, the compounding effect of consistent effort leads to success. Whether it's investing a little more each month, continually refining a business model, or improving a skill, the cumulative effect of these actions is far more powerful than sporadic efforts.

- Reinforcing Good Habits: Consistency helps reinforce the habits that lead to success. By practicing the same positive actions regularly, millionaires engrain these habits into their lifestyle, making them second nature. Over time, these habits form the bedrock of their achievements.

- Staying on Track with Long-Term Goals: Consistency ensures that millionaires stay aligned with their long-term vision, even when the day-to-day progress seems slow. By committing to consistent action, they avoid getting sidetracked by distractions, setbacks, or the temptation to quit.

Cultivating Discipline and Consistency

Discipline and consistency are the pillars of success for millionaires. While others may struggle with staying on track or lose focus when results aren't immediate, millionaires build their fortunes by consistently following through on disciplined actions day after day.

By establishing productive daily routines, mastering time management, and sticking to their long-term plans, millionaires set themselves up for sustained success. As you work toward your own financial goals, remember that it's not about being perfect or making grand leaps in progress. It's about showing up each day, doing the work, and letting the power of discipline and consistency work in your favor.

While motivation may fluctuate, disciplined individuals maintain a steady commitment to their goals regardless of how they feel on any given day. Successful people recognize that consistent, small efforts over time lead to extraordinary results. The daily habits they establish—waking up early, prioritizing tasks, and following routines—allow them to make progress even when faced with distractions or challenges. This relentless discipline creates momentum, ensuring that they stay on track to achieve their long-term vision.

A prime example of discipline and consistency is Jeff Bezos, the founder of Amazon. Early in Amazon's history, Bezos was unwavering in his disciplined focus on customer satisfaction. Even as the company struggled in its early years, he consistently followed through on his strategy of offering a wide selection of products, fast delivery, and low prices. Bezos maintained a disciplined approach to reinvesting profits back into the business instead of focusing on short-term gains, which helped Amazon grow into the global giant it is today. His daily commitment to operational excellence and innovation, without getting distracted by external noise, was key to Amazon's monumental success.

Consistency doesn't just apply to business strategies, but also to personal habits that millionaires cultivate. For example, many highly successful individuals, like Tony Robbins and Richard Branson, have rigorous morning routines that they follow without fail. These routines often involve physical exercise, meditation, and reviewing their goals for the day. By starting each day with discipline, they set the tone for a productive and focused day ahead. The key is that they don't wait for inspiration or motivation to act; they rely on their habits and discipline to propel them forward.

To apply this habit of discipline and consistency in your own life, it's important to create non-negotiable routines, develop self-discipline by doing difficult tasks first, and remain focused on your long-term goals. Even when results aren't immediate, trust the process, because consistent effort will compound over time, leading to success.

Millionaires are driven to have discipline and consistency by several key factors that set them apart from the average person. These motivating forces fuel their determination to stay on track and maintain focus on their goals, even when the journey is difficult or the results aren't immediately visible.

1. Clear Vision and Purpose

One of the primary drivers for a millionaire's discipline is their clear vision and sense of purpose. Successful individuals are often deeply committed to a bigger goal or mission that excites them and gives their actions meaning. Whether it's building a business, achieving financial independence, or making an impact on the world, this clear sense of purpose motivates them to maintain discipline. Their vision becomes a guiding force that pushes them to stay consistent, even when the process is challenging or mundane. Having a long-term vision makes it easier to make sacrifices in the short term, as they know every small effort is a step toward their larger goal.

2. Desire for Freedom and Control

Many millionaires are driven by the desire for financial freedom and control over their lives. Discipline and consistency are essential to achieving and maintaining that freedom. By being disciplined with their time, finances, and decisions, they can create a life where they are not dependent on others for income or resources. This desire to be in control of their own destiny fuels their determination to stick to routines, manage their investments wisely, and make smart financial decisions. The thought of living a life free from financial constraints and having the freedom to pursue their passions is a powerful motivator.

3. Fear of Failure or Losing Success

Another motivator for discipline among millionaires is the fear of losing what they've worked so hard to achieve. Many self-made millionaires have experienced hardship, failures, or financial struggles before attaining their success, and they are driven to avoid falling back into those situations. The fear of failure or losing their financial standing often pushes them to remain disciplined in maintaining their wealth, growing their businesses, and managing risks. They understand that complacency can lead to setbacks, so they stay committed to their routines, keep learning, and consistently improve to protect and expand their success.

These internal drivers—having a clear vision, craving freedom, and a healthy fear of failure—help millionaires cultivate the discipline and consistency needed to achieve and sustain their success over time.

CHAPTER 03

THE HABIT OF CONTINUOUS LEARING

One of the defining habits of millionaires is their commitment to continuous learning. Success in any field requires more than just hard work and determination; it also demands a constant acquisition of knowledge. Millionaires are lifelong learners, continually seeking ways to improve themselves, stay ahead of trends, and expand their skill sets. This relentless pursuit of knowledge keeps them at the forefront of their industries and helps them navigate the complexities of wealth creation and management.

In this chapter, we will explore how millionaires prioritize education, whether through formal means like degrees or self-directed study. We will also discuss how they stay informed about their industries, the economy, and global trends, as well as the vital role of mentorship and networking in their personal and professional development.

The Value of Continuous Learning

The world is constantly evolving, and millionaires understand that staying stagnant can lead to falling behind. Lifelong learning helps them stay adaptable and competitive in ever-changing markets. The most successful individuals never believe they know everything—rather, they see every day as an opportunity to learn something new.

Continuous learning does more than enhance knowledge; it also builds resilience and fosters creativity. Millionaires who embrace a growth mindset—the belief that abilities and intelligence can be developed through dedication and hard work—are more likely to take risks, overcome challenges, and pursue new opportunities.

Formal Education vs. Self-Study

While some millionaires have advanced degrees from prestigious universities, many others have achieved success through self-directed learning. Both pathways have their merits, but what they share is a commitment to gaining knowledge, whether in a structured academic environment or through personal exploration.

- Formal Education: Some millionaires invest in traditional education by obtaining degrees in fields like business, finance, law, or engineering. Formal education provides a solid foundation of knowledge, a structured learning environment, and networking opportunities. However, many millionaires go beyond their initial schooling, pursuing continuing education programs, attending executive seminars, or taking specialized courses to keep their skills relevant and sharp.

- Self-Study: Many millionaires, particularly those who are self-made, attribute their success to self-directed learning. They are voracious readers and researchers, constantly seeking out books, articles, podcasts, and other resources that help them expand their knowledge. This approach allows them to tailor their education to their specific interests and needs, giving them an edge in their industries.

Regardless of the educational path, the common thread is that millionaires never stop learning. They view education as an ongoing process rather than a finite achievement.

Reading as a Cornerstone of Learning

One of the most common habits shared by millionaires is their love of reading. Books are a treasure trove of knowledge, offering insights from successful individuals, historical events, and innovative ideas. Reading helps millionaires learn from the successes and failures of others, broadening their perspectives and equipping them with new strategies for success.

Warren Buffett, one of the wealthiest people in the world, famously spends five to six hours a day reading newspapers, financial reports, and books. He attributes much of his success to this habit, often recommending others to read 500 pages a day. Similarly, Bill Gates is known to read around 50 books a year, believing that reading gives him an opportunity to explore new subjects and improve his understanding of the world.

Millionaires often focus on books in areas such as:

- Business and Finance: Books about entrepreneurship, leadership, investing, and economics help them understand how to build wealth and navigate the complexities of business.

- Self-Improvement: Books on psychology, habits, and personal development provide tools for enhancing productivity, discipline, and mental well-being.

- Biographies and Case Studies: Learning from the lives of other successful individuals gives millionaires valuable lessons in perseverance, decision-making, and innovation.

Reading provides a way for millionaires to continuously feed their minds with new ideas and solutions, often inspiring creative approaches to their own businesses and investments.

Attending Seminars and Conferences

Beyond books, millionaires invest in attending seminars, workshops, and conferences. These events provide an opportunity to learn from experts in various fields, engage in discussions about industry trends, and gain insights into new technologies, strategies, and ideas.

Seminars and conferences also offer networking opportunities, allowing millionaires to connect with other successful individuals who share their passion for growth and learning. By attending these events, they can ask questions, seek advice, and learn from the experiences of others in their industry.

Many successful individuals make it a point to attend at least a few high-profile events each year, whether it's an industry-specific conference, a leadership summit, or a seminar on personal development. These gatherings serve as a platform for continued learning and staying ahead of the curve.

The Importance of Networking

Networking is one of the most valuable forms of learning for millionaires. Building relationships with other successful individuals gives them access to a wealth of knowledge, resources, and opportunities. Through networking, millionaires can learn from the experiences of others, gain new perspectives, and collaborate on projects that accelerate their success.

Millionaires often cultivate relationships with mentors, advisors, peers, and colleagues who challenge them to think differently and push them to grow. They recognize that no one achieves success in isolation, and that leveraging the collective wisdom of a strong network can open doors to new opportunities.

Seeking Mentorship

Mentorship is another critical aspect of continuous learning for millionaires. Having a mentor provides guidance, support, and feedback from someone who has already achieved a high level of success. Mentors help millionaires navigate challenges, make better decisions, and avoid common pitfalls.

Many millionaires actively seek out mentors who have experience in areas they wish to improve or expand. This relationship is mutually beneficial, as mentors also gain new insights from mentoring and often build lasting connections with their mentees.

Whether formal or informal, mentorship helps millionaires accelerate their learning curve, providing them with the knowledge and strategies they need to overcome challenges and reach new heights.

Staying Informed About Industry and Economic Trends

In today's fast-paced world, staying informed about industry and economic trends is crucial for success. Millionaires make it a priority to stay up to date on developments in their industries and the broader economy. This allows them to anticipate changes, capitalize on emerging opportunities, and avoid potential risks.

Here's how millionaires stay informed:

- Reading Industry Publications: Millionaires regularly consume trade journals, business magazines, and industry-specific news outlets to stay informed about the latest trends and innovations in their fields.

- Following Market News: They stay attuned to financial markets and economic reports, ensuring they are aware of fluctuations in interest rates, inflation, and global economic trends that might impact their investments or business ventures.

- Listening to Experts: Many millionaires follow thought leaders, economists, and market analysts, seeking insights that help them make informed decisions.

By staying informed, millionaires can make strategic decisions that keep them ahead of the competition, allowing them to adapt quickly to changing circumstances and capitalize on emerging opportunities.

The Mindset of a Lifelong Learner

At the core of continuous learning is a growth mindset. Millionaires believe that learning is a lifelong journey, not a destination. They are curious, open to new ideas, and unafraid to challenge their own assumptions. This mindset drives them to seek out new knowledge, skills, and experiences, ensuring that they continue to grow both personally and professionally.

Learning is not just about acquiring new information but about applying it in ways that enhance their lives and businesses. Millionaires who adopt a growth mindset are more likely to take risks, innovate, and persevere in the face of challenges.

Conclusion: Embrace Learning to Unlock Success

The habit of continuous learning is a cornerstone of millionaire success. Whether through formal education, self-study, mentorship, or staying informed about industry trends, millionaires understand that knowledge is power. By committing to lifelong learning, they equip themselves with the tools they need to adapt, grow, and succeed in an ever-changing world.

Why is the habit of continuous learning imperative in the millionaire's mindset?

The habit of continuous learning is imperative in the millionaire mindset because it ensures that successful individuals remain adaptable, competitive, and informed in an ever-changing world. Millionaires understand that knowledge is power, and in today's fast-paced, technology-driven economy, staying stagnant can lead to irrelevance. The most successful people recognize that no matter how much they know, there is always more to learn—new strategies to explore, emerging technologies to master, and evolving market trends to understand. By continuously seeking knowledge, they position themselves to seize opportunities and navigate challenges with confidence and foresight.

One of the key reasons continuous learning is so vital to millionaires is the need to stay ahead of the competition. In business, industries evolve rapidly, and those who stop learning risk falling behind. A prime example of the importance of ongoing learning is Bill Gates, who despite being one of the wealthiest individuals in the world, devotes significant time each year to reading books across a wide range of subjects. Gates credits much of his success to his insatiable curiosity and desire to learn. Whether it's understanding global issues, scientific advancements, or new business innovations, Gates keeps learning to remain at the forefront of his field. His investment in continuous education allows him to stay innovative and make strategic decisions that contribute to the growth of Microsoft and his philanthropic endeavors.

Additionally, the ability to learn from failure and adapt is a critical reason millionaires embrace lifelong learning. They understand that setbacks and challenges are inevitable, but by maintaining a growth mindset and learning from mistakes, they can pivot and find new paths to success. Sara Blakely, the founder of Spanx, often shares how her failures and willingness to learn from them played a pivotal role in her entrepreneurial journey. Blakely, who initially struggled to get her product noticed, continually sought feedback and adjusted her approach. Her commitment to learning from mistakes, improving her product, and refining her business strategies helped her turn Spanx into a billion-dollar company.

Therefore, continuous learning is not just a habit but a mindset that millionaires cultivate to remain relevant, innovate, and excel in their industries. Whether through reading, attending seminars, or seeking mentorship, millionaires understand that their growth depends on their willingness to learn and adapt. By committing to a lifetime of learning, they ensure that they are always prepared to capitalize on opportunities, solve complex problems, and lead with knowledge and expertise.

The danger of "lack of knowledge"

The phrase "lack of knowledge makes people perish" emphasizes the critical importance of understanding and wisdom in achieving success and avoiding failure. This idea, often rooted in spiritual, historical, and practical teachings, highlights several key reasons why ignorance or a lack of knowledge can lead to one's downfall:

1. Inability to Make Informed Decisions

When people lack knowledge, they are more likely to make poor decisions based on incomplete or inaccurate information. In both personal and professional contexts, making uninformed choices can lead to financial loss, missed opportunities, and even personal harm. Knowledge empowers individuals to assess situations carefully, weigh the pros and cons, and make informed, strategic decisions. Without it, they may act impulsively or fall prey to poor advice, leading to negative outcomes.

For example, individuals who lack financial literacy may struggle with budgeting, investing, or managing debt, which can lead to financial ruin. Conversely, those who invest in learning about money management are more likely to build wealth, avoid debt, and make smart investment choices. Knowledge gives people the tools to navigate life's complexities and avoid pitfalls.

2. Vulnerability to Manipulation and Exploitation

A lack of knowledge often leaves individuals vulnerable to manipulation, deception, or exploitation by others who may take advantage of their ignorance. Whether in business, politics, or personal relationships, those who are uninformed can be easily misled by false promises, scams, or unethical practices. Knowledge provides the defense needed to critically analyze information, ask the right questions, and protect oneself from being exploited.

In the digital age, this has become even more relevant. People who lack basic knowledge about cybersecurity, for example, are more prone to falling victim to phishing scams or identity theft. Similarly, in business, entrepreneurs who lack understanding of legal contracts or market trends may be taken advantage of by competitors or dishonest partners.

3. Failure to Adapt and Grow

In a rapidly changing world, the ability to continuously learn and adapt is crucial for survival and success. A lack of knowledge often leads to stagnation, where individuals or businesses fail to innovate, grow, or keep pace with advancements in technology, industry trends, or personal development. Those who stop learning become obsolete, unable to compete with others who are constantly evolving and staying informed.

This is particularly evident in industries disrupted by technology, where companies that fail to innovate and learn new strategies—such as Blockbuster in the face of Netflix—have perished. On a personal level, failing to grow and adapt in one's career can result in missed promotions, job loss, or the inability to achieve long-term goals.

In essence, lack of knowledge leads to perishing because it leaves individuals ill-equipped to navigate life's challenges, make informed choices, protect themselves from harm, and grow with the times. Continuous learning and the pursuit of wisdom are vital to flourishing in both the practical and spiritual aspects of life.

CHAPTER 04

RISK TAKING AND DECISION MAKING

One of the critical factors that sets millionaires apart from others is their ability to take calculated risks and make informed decisions. Contrary to the misconception that wealthy individuals avoid risk, millionaires understand that risk is an inherent part of any path to success. However, they approach risk differently: they assess it strategically, act with confidence, and know when to trust their intuition. They are not reckless but rather skilled in balancing risk and reward in ways that maximize their chances for success.

In this chapter, we will delve into how millionaires approach risk-taking, make decisions under pressure, learn from their failures, and leverage intuition in their decision-making processes.

The Nature of Calculated Risks

Risk is often seen as a gamble, but successful individuals take calculated risks, meaning they thoroughly assess potential outcomes before committing to a decision. They weigh the benefits and downsides, making sure the risks they take are aligned with their long-term goals and values.

Calculated risks are based on informed decisions, where millionaires consider factors like:

- Potential Return: What is the upside of this decision? How significant could the rewards be if it succeeds?

- Likelihood of Success: What are the chances of this risk paying off? How much control do I have over the outcome?

- Downside Risk: What is the worst-case scenario? Am I willing to accept the consequences if the decision doesn't work out?

- Risk Mitigation: How can I minimize the potential downsides or manage the risk more effectively?

Millionaires don't shy away from risks, but they ensure that they fully understand the potential consequences before making a move. They know that while there are no guarantees in life, minimizing unnecessary risks and taking well-thought-out risks is key to building wealth.

Risk and Innovation: Breaking the Mold

Many millionaires are pioneers and innovators, and innovation inherently involves risk. Whether it's launching a new business, entering a new market, or developing a new product, these endeavors carry uncertainty. However, millionaires embrace these opportunities because they understand that significant rewards often come from uncharted territory.

Risk-taking drives innovation, and millionaires are willing to be bold in areas where others might hesitate. Take for example Jeff Bezos, who took a substantial risk by leaving his well-established career to start Amazon, an e-commerce company that at the time seemed risky in the nascent days of the internet. His willingness to break the mold and try something new ultimately revolutionized retail and made him one of the wealthiest individuals in the world.

Millionaires know that staying in the comfort zone rarely leads to extraordinary success. They are willing to take risks, recognizing that failure is a possible outcome, but the rewards of success outweigh the fear of failure.

Making Decisions Under Pressure

Millionaires often operate in high-stakes environments where they must make critical decisions under pressure. In these moments, they rely on a combination of experience, data, and intuition to guide their choices. Making decisions in stressful situations requires a calm mind, an ability to quickly analyze information, and the confidence to act decisively.

Here's how millionaires navigate decision-making under pressure:

- Relying on Data: Successful individuals gather as much relevant information as possible before making decisions. Whether it's financial data, market research, or advice from trusted advisors, they use data to guide their choices. However, they don't get paralyzed by analysis. Once they have enough information, they make a decision rather than endlessly seeking more data.

- Breaking Down Decisions: When faced with overwhelming decisions, millionaires break them down into manageable steps. This method allows them to tackle smaller parts of the problem, reducing the pressure of making one massive decision all at once. By focusing on incremental choices, they can adjust as they go rather than committing to an all-or-nothing decision.

- Practicing Emotional Control: High-pressure situations can lead to emotional decision-making, which often results in poor outcomes. Millionaires practice emotional control and mindfulness to stay calm and objective. They don't let fear or excitement cloud their judgment, instead focusing on logical, well-thought-out choices.

- Making Decisive Moves: Indecision can be more detrimental than making the wrong decision. Millionaires are known for their ability to make decisions quickly and confidently, even when they don't have all the answers. They trust that they can course-correct if necessary, but they avoid wasting time by hesitating or second-guessing themselves.

Learning from Failure

No one is immune to failure, not even the most successful millionaires. However, what sets them apart is their approach to failure. Instead of seeing it as a setback, they view failure as a learning opportunity. They analyze what went wrong, extract valuable lessons, and apply those insights to future decisions.

Here's how millionaires learn from failure:

- Failure as Feedback: Millionaires understand that failure is part of the process, and they use it as feedback to refine their strategies. Rather than letting failure discourage them, they analyze it to understand what went wrong and how they can avoid similar mistakes in the future.

- Failing Fast: Some millionaires adopt a "fail fast" mentality, meaning they prefer to experiment and take risks early, allowing them to quickly determine whether a strategy works or not. This approach helps them avoid wasting time and resources on ideas that won't succeed, allowing them to pivot and try something new.

- Resilience: Millionaires develop resilience by bouncing back quickly from failure. They don't dwell on mistakes or let setbacks define them. Instead, they use these experiences to build their confidence, knowing that each failure brings them one step closer to success.

- Risk Management: While millionaires are willing to take risks, they also know how to manage failure. They never risk more than they are willing to lose, and they always have contingency plans in place to minimize the damage if things don't go as expected.

Trusting Intuition

While data and analysis are critical, millionaires also understand the importance of intuition in decision-making. Intuition is the ability to understand something instinctively, without the need for conscious reasoning. It is often developed through experience, pattern recognition, and a deep understanding of one's industry or market.

Here's how millionaires use intuition effectively:

- Experience-Based Intuition: After years of experience in their fields, millionaires develop an intuitive sense of what works and what doesn't. They can recognize patterns in business, investing, or market trends that others might miss, allowing them to make decisions based on their gut feelings.

- Balancing Logic with Intuition: While millionaires trust their intuition, they don't rely on it blindly. They balance intuition with logic and data, using both to guide their decision-making. When intuition aligns with solid data, they act confidently. When it conflicts, they take a step back to reassess the situation.

- Knowing When to Trust Their Gut: Millionaires are selective about when to trust their gut feelings. They often rely on intuition when there isn't enough concrete information available or when they need to make decisions in unfamiliar situations. However, they also know when to seek advice or more data before making a choice.

Examples of Risk-Taking Millionaires

1. Elon Musk: Musk's decision to invest nearly all of his PayPal earnings into Tesla and SpaceX was a massive financial risk, especially when both companies faced early struggles. However, Musk's confidence in his vision and willingness to take such a bold risk eventually paid off, as both companies have become industry leaders.

2. Richard Branson: The founder of the Virgin Group has taken countless risks throughout his career, from launching Virgin Atlantic to venturing into space tourism with

Virgin Galactic. Branson's risk-taking is calculated—he gathers information, surrounds himself with a strong team, and backs his ventures with a willingness to fail and learn from it.

3. Sara Blakely: The founder of Spanx took a personal risk by investing her life savings into her product idea. Despite initial rejection from manufacturers and retailers, she trusted her instincts and kept pushing forward. Her calculated risk paid off, and Spanx became a multimillion-dollar company.

Mastering Risk and Decision-Making

Millionaires don't achieve success by playing it safe. They understand that taking calculated risks is essential for growth, and they are confident in their decision-making processes, even under pressure. By learning from failure, balancing data with intuition, and acting decisively, they set themselves up for long-term success.

Quantitative Risk Management and decision making in Millionaires

In addition to intuition and boldness, millionaires often employ quantitative risk management to make calculated decisions that minimize potential losses and maximize gains. This analytical approach to assessing risk involves using data, models, and probability to evaluate the potential outcomes of a decision, ensuring that their choices are informed and strategic. Unlike reckless risk-takers, successful individuals leverage numbers and information to make well-informed decisions, especially when it comes to financial investments, business ventures, or entering new markets.

Quantitative risk management involves gathering and analyzing data to understand the likelihood of different scenarios. For instance, before making a significant investment, millionaires assess market trends, evaluate the financial performance of potential investments, and consider the risks of failure based on past data. They often use risk metrics like Value at Risk (VaR), which calculates the potential loss in an investment over a given time frame under normal market conditions. This allows them to quantify the risk they are taking and make decisions with a clear understanding of the possible downsides. This approach ensures that they aren't simply gambling with their resources but are instead making educated decisions to protect their wealth.

For example, Warren Buffett, one of the most successful investors, is known for his careful analysis of businesses before investing in them. Buffett evaluates a company's financial health, market position, and long-term potential using quantitative data. He doesn't take unnecessary risks but chooses investments where he can predict a high likelihood of steady returns. This method of applying risk management ensures that his decisions are based on measurable facts rather than gut feeling alone. Through this disciplined approach, Buffett has managed to consistently make sound investments and avoid catastrophic losses that come from poorly informed decisions.

Another aspect of quantitative risk management is scenario analysis, where millionaires assess different possible outcomes of a decision, including best-case, worst-case, and most-likely scenarios. This allows them to visualize the full range of possible outcomes and plan for contingencies. By understanding the spectrum of risks, they can put safeguards in place—such as setting stop-loss orders in stock trading or diversifying their investment portfolios. This analytical mindset ensures that even if the worst-case scenario occurs, the impact is manageable and does not derail their long-term financial goals.

In conclusion, millionaires' ability to make bold yet calculated decisions is not based on luck or intuition alone. They employ sophisticated risk management techniques, using quantitative data to assess and mitigate potential dangers. By mastering these techniques, they are able to take informed risks that lead to sustainable growth, knowing they've prepared for possible setbacks. This combination of quantitative risk management and decision-making gives them the edge needed to thrive in competitive markets while preserving their wealth for the long term.

This reliance on quantitative risk management also ties into the discipline and consistency discussed in earlier chapters. Millionaires develop systems and frameworks to regularly assess the risks associated with their ventures, investments, and financial decisions. They don't approach risk-taking haphazardly; instead, they establish processes to monitor and adjust their strategies based on new data, market fluctuations, and performance outcomes. By doing so, they minimize emotional decision-making and remove biases that could cloud their judgment.

For example, in the world of stock trading or entrepreneurship, millionaires often use tools such as risk-reward ratios to determine whether a particular investment is worth pursuing. This involves comparing the potential return of an investment against the amount of risk it carries. If the expected reward significantly outweighs the potential risk, the decision becomes clearer, allowing the millionaire to proceed with confidence. This methodical approach creates a roadmap for making sound decisions, even when there's uncertainty involved.

Moreover, portfolio diversification is another key concept in quantitative risk management that millionaires rely on. By spreading investments across different asset classes—such as stocks, bonds, real estate, and businesses—they reduce the risk associated with any one investment's poor performance. This is a calculated move to safeguard wealth while still seeking growth. Many successful individuals adopt a strategy known as Modern Portfolio Theory (MPT), which involves selecting a variety of investments that are not strongly correlated, ensuring that losses in one area are offset by gains in another. This balanced, data-driven approach reflects how millionaires use sophisticated risk management to maintain stability while achieving consistent financial growth.

In conclusion, millionaires' approach to risk-taking is a carefully honed balance between ambition and caution. They recognize that taking risks is necessary for achieving extraordinary success, but they do so in a way that limits potential downsides. By using quantitative tools such as risk-reward ratios, scenario analysis, and portfolio diversification, they transform risk from a reckless gamble into a manageable and strategic component of decision-making. This mindset allows them to take advantage of opportunities that others might shy away from, all while protecting themselves from the financial pitfalls that can derail those without a plan.

Quantitative risk management is a cornerstone of their success, and it can be adopted by anyone willing to apply the same level of rigor and foresight in their own decision-making.

CHAPTER 05

RESILIENCE AND ADAPTABILITY

In the journey to financial success, setbacks are inevitable. However, what distinguishes millionaires from the rest is their remarkable resilience and adaptability. These individuals don't let challenges derail them; instead, they use adversity as fuel for growth and innovation. Resilience is the ability to recover quickly from difficulties, while adaptability is the skill of adjusting to new conditions. Together, these traits enable millionaires to navigate unpredictable environments and thrive in the face of adversity.

In this chapter, we will explore how millionaires demonstrate resilience, adapt to change, and leverage challenges as stepping stones to greater success. We'll also examine the role of mental toughness and emotional intelligence in maintaining resilience, and how these qualities help millionaires stay focused and motivated, even when faced with setbacks.

The Nature of Resilience

Resilience is not about avoiding failure or setbacks; it's about how individuals respond when things go wrong. Millionaires understand that failure is a part of life and business, and they develop the mental and emotional strength to bounce back from disappointments. Rather than being overwhelmed by setbacks, they see them as temporary obstacles and remain committed to their long-term goals.

Resilient individuals don't give up when they encounter challenges. Instead, they assess the situation, learn from it, and pivot when necessary. This mindset allows them to view failure as a valuable learning experience rather than a personal or professional defeat.

Recovering from Failure

Millionaires often experience failures on their path to success. Whether it's a failed business, a poor investment, or a personal setback, they don't dwell on their losses. Instead, they recover quickly by taking the following actions:

- Learning from Mistakes: Millionaires see failure as a teacher. They analyze what went wrong, why it happened, and how they can avoid making the same mistake in the future.

This reflective process allows them to gain insights from their failures and turn them into opportunities for growth.

- Embracing a Growth Mindset: A growth mindset, the belief that abilities and intelligence can be developed through effort, is a key trait of resilient individuals. Millionaires with a growth mindset view setbacks as a natural part of the learning process. They understand that failure is not a reflection of their worth, but a necessary step toward eventual success.

- Moving Forward Quickly: Instead of dwelling on failure, millionaires shift their focus to the next opportunity. They don't let disappointment paralyze them. By taking swift action after a setback, they regain momentum and maintain progress toward their goals.

For example, Henry Ford, one of the most iconic figures in American business history, experienced multiple failed business ventures before eventually founding Ford Motor Company. Rather than giving up, Ford learned from his early failures and used them to refine his business approach, ultimately revolutionizing the automobile industry.

Adaptability: Thriving in Change

Adaptability is the ability to adjust to new circumstances, whether they involve technological changes, market fluctuations, or personal shifts. In an ever-evolving world, millionaires are highly adaptable, constantly adjusting their strategies and approaches to stay ahead of the curve. They understand that rigidity is the enemy of growth and that success often requires flexibility.

Here's how millionaires demonstrate adaptability:

- Embracing Change: While many people resist change, millionaires actively embrace it. They see change as an opportunity to innovate, improve, and gain a competitive edge. Whether it's adopting new technologies, exploring new markets, or adjusting business models, millionaires are quick to adapt when the situation calls for it.

- Pivoting When Necessary: When millionaires encounter challenges that disrupt their original plans, they don't hesitate to pivot. Pivoting means making a significant change in direction to take advantage of new opportunities or overcome unexpected obstacles. By remaining flexible and open to change, millionaires can find new paths to success when their initial strategies don't work.

- Staying Informed: Adaptability requires staying informed about industry trends, market conditions, and technological advancements. Millionaires make it a priority to keep up with the latest developments in their fields, ensuring that they are prepared to adapt when necessary.

For instance, Steve Jobs was a master of adaptability. After being ousted from Apple, the company he co-founded,

Jobs could have let the setback define him. Instead, he adapted by founding NeXT and acquiring Pixar, which eventually became one of the most successful animation studios. When he returned to Apple, Jobs applied the lessons he learned to transform Apple into one of the most valuable companies in the world.

Using Adversity as a Stepping Stone

Millionaires don't just survive adversity; they use it as a catalyst for growth. They recognize that the most significant opportunities often arise from difficult circumstances. When faced with challenges, they look for ways to turn adversity into an advantage.

Here's how millionaires turn challenges into stepping stones for success:

- Innovating Through Adversity: Many millionaires use difficult situations as inspiration to innovate. For example, when economic conditions or industry disruptions create obstacles, they find creative solutions that not only help them survive but also thrive. Adversity forces them to think outside the box and find new ways to add value to the market.

- Building Mental Toughness: Adversity helps millionaires develop mental toughness—the ability to stay focused, positive, and persistent in the face of difficulty. Mental toughness allows them to keep pushing forward, even when the odds are stacked against them.

- Strengthening Their Resolve: Challenges often strengthen a millionaire's determination to succeed. By overcoming adversity, they build confidence in their ability to handle whatever comes their way. Each challenge they face reinforces their belief that they can achieve their goals, no matter the circumstances.

The Role of Mental Toughness

Mental toughness is the ability to remain strong, focused, and driven, even when facing difficult situations. Millionaires possess this quality in abundance, which helps them stay on track despite setbacks, failures, and uncertainties. Mental toughness is not something people are born with; it's a skill that can be developed through practice and perseverance.

Here's how millionaires cultivate mental toughness:

- Maintaining Focus on Long-Term Goals: Millionaires don't let short-term setbacks distract them from their long-term vision. They stay focused on their ultimate goals, even when the journey becomes difficult. This long-term perspective helps them keep their emotions in check and stay committed to the path ahead.

- Practicing Patience: Success doesn't happen overnight, and millionaires understand that the journey to wealth requires patience. Mental toughness involves staying patient and persistent, knowing that their efforts will pay off in the future, even if they don't see immediate results.

- Developing Emotional Control: Mental toughness requires emotional intelligence—the ability to manage emotions effectively. Millionaires don't let fear, frustration, or anger dictate their decisions. Instead, they remain calm and composed, even in high-pressure situations, allowing them to make rational choices and avoid impulsive reactions.

Emotional Intelligence and Resilience

Emotional intelligence (EQ) plays a crucial role in resilience. EQ is the ability to recognize, understand, and manage emotions in oneself and others. It enables millionaires to navigate the emotional ups and downs of their journey, building strong relationships and making sound decisions under pressure.

Here's how emotional intelligence supports resilience:

- Self-Awareness: Millionaires are highly self-aware, meaning they understand their strengths, weaknesses, and emotional triggers. This self-awareness allows them to manage their emotions and stay composed, even in challenging situations. It also helps them recognize when they need to seek help or advice, preventing burnout.

- Empathy: Successful individuals often demonstrate high levels of empathy—the ability to understand the emotions of others. This helps them build strong connections with employees, business partners, and clients. Empathy also allows them to navigate conflicts and challenges with greater emotional intelligence, which strengthens their ability to adapt and recover from setbacks.

- Managing Stress: Emotional intelligence helps millionaires manage stress effectively. By understanding their emotions and using stress management techniques—such as mindfulness, exercise, or meditation—they can prevent stress from overwhelming them and maintain resilience during tough times.

Building Resilience and Adaptability

Resilience and adaptability are critical traits for anyone aspiring to become a millionaire. By developing mental toughness, embracing change, and turning adversity into opportunity, millionaires consistently find ways to overcome challenges and keep moving toward their goals. These qualities allow them to remain confident, focused, and resourceful, no matter what life throws their way.

Resilience and adaptability in leadership

Resilience and adaptability are not only personal traits of successful millionaires but also essential qualities in leadership. In today's fast-paced and constantly changing business landscape, leaders must not only be resilient and adaptable themselves but also foster these traits in their teams. Leadership in times of uncertainty requires the ability to respond to challenges swiftly, pivot strategies when necessary, and maintain focus in the face of adversity. Millionaires who excel in leadership know how to cultivate these traits within their organizations, ensuring that their teams are prepared to navigate any disruptions or challenges that arise.

Targeted training plays a crucial role in developing resilience and adaptability in teams. It equips employees with the tools and mindset needed to face setbacks and changes in the workplace. Such training typically includes crisis management exercises, problem-solving workshops, and emotional intelligence development. Through these activities, team members learn how to handle stress, approach problems creatively, and adapt to new circumstances with confidence. Leaders who prioritize this type of training create an environment where setbacks are viewed as learning opportunities rather than reasons for panic. They prepare their teams to bounce back from failures and quickly adapt to new realities, such as shifts in market demands, technological advancements, or internal restructuring.

A prime example of how targeted training can build resilience and adaptability can be seen in companies that focus on continuous learning and skill development. Organizations like Google and Amazon invest heavily in training programs designed to encourage employees to stay ahead of industry trends and develop a growth mindset. These programs emphasize the importance of staying flexible in the face of change, teaching employees to embrace new technologies and adapt to shifting priorities. This culture of adaptability has allowed these companies to maintain their leadership positions in highly competitive and evolving markets. By fostering an environment of resilience and continuous improvement, leaders ensure that their teams are not only capable of handling disruptions but also thrive in them.

Furthermore, leaders who encourage resilience and adaptability within their teams often see an increase in employee engagement, creativity, and innovation. When employees are equipped with the skills to adapt to change, they feel more empowered to take risks, suggest new ideas, and contribute to the overall success of the organization. Resilient teams are better positioned to take calculated risks, learn from mistakes, and continuously improve, ultimately driving business growth. In contrast, teams lacking these qualities tend to stagnate or struggle to cope with the pressures of a rapidly changing environment, leading to decreased productivity and morale.

In summary, resilience and adaptability are indispensable traits for leaders aiming to succeed in today's dynamic world. Through targeted training, leaders can cultivate these traits within their teams, enabling them to respond effectively to challenges, innovate under pressure, and stay competitive in an ever-evolving workplace. This proactive approach to developing resilient and adaptable teams ensures long-term success and prepares organizations to handle whatever uncertainties the future may hold.

In addition to fostering resilience and adaptability through training, effective leadership also involves creating a culture that encourages open communication and flexibility. Leaders who maintain transparent lines of communication with their teams enable members to express concerns, offer suggestions, and voice any challenges they face. This openness helps employees feel supported when adapting to new situations or when facing difficulties, knowing their leadership is responsive and willing to listen. When employees feel empowered to share their experiences, leaders can address issues more quickly and provide tailored support, reinforcing both resilience and adaptability.

Moreover, adaptability in leadership often involves encouraging a growth mindset within the team. Leaders who model a growth mindset—an attitude that focuses on learning, effort, and persistence—show their teams that setbacks and challenges are part of the process. This is particularly important when changes in the workplace, such as technological advancements or organizational restructuring, require people to learn new skills or adjust their roles. By cultivating a growth mindset, leaders emphasize that obstacles are opportunities to develop and improve, rather than reasons to retreat or give up.

Organizations like Microsoft have successfully implemented a growth mindset at every level, driven by CEO Satya Nadella's leadership philosophy. Under Nadella, Microsoft's culture shifted from a "know-it-all" mindset to a "learn-it-all" one, where employees are encouraged to embrace challenges and continuous learning. This has not only boosted the company's innovation but also made its teams more adaptable to market changes and technological disruptions. By instilling resilience and adaptability as part of the corporate culture, Microsoft has been able to navigate complex transformations, like the shift to cloud computing, and sustain long-term success.

Finally, resilience and adaptability are essential for preparing teams for the future of work, where flexibility and the ability to pivot quickly will be key determinants of success. As new technologies such as artificial intelligence (AI) and automation reshape industries, leaders must ensure that their teams are equipped to embrace these changes. Investing in skill-building programs and promoting a culture of lifelong learning will help employees remain relevant and adaptable as job roles evolve. In industries where disruption is frequent, like tech or finance, having a resilient workforce ready to learn and adjust ensures that the organization remains competitive and innovative in the face of change.

In conclusion, resilience and adaptability are critical traits for leadership, especially in the fast-evolving modern workplace. By investing in targeted training, promoting a growth mindset, and fostering open communication, leaders can develop resilient teams that are not only capable of handling adversity but also thrive in the midst of change. As industries continue to evolve, the ability to adapt will be one of the key drivers of long-term success for both leaders and their teams.

CHAPTER 06

NETWORKING AND RELATIONSHIP

The saying, "your network is your net worth," holds profound truth for millionaires. Building wealth and success is not a solitary pursuit; it requires the support, insights, and collaboration of others. Millionaires understand the power of relationships, not just for financial gain but for personal growth and long-term success. They are deliberate about who they connect with, understanding that the right relationships can open doors, create opportunities, and provide valuable resources.

In this chapter, we will explore how millionaires build and maintain strong professional and personal relationships. We will examine the value of networking, the importance of giving before receiving, and why it's critical to surround oneself with like-minded, ambitious individuals. Networking is not just about meeting people; it's about fostering genuine, mutually beneficial connections that help individuals grow personally and professionally.

The Value of Networking

Networking is one of the most powerful tools for success. Whether it's meeting potential business partners, investors, mentors, or customers, building a strong network creates opportunities that would otherwise be inaccessible. Millionaires prioritize networking because they understand that success often depends on who you know, not just what you know.

Networking offers several key benefits:

- Access to Opportunities: Many opportunities are never publicly advertised or available to the general public. Millionaires who network effectively gain access to these hidden opportunities through personal relationships. Whether it's a lucrative investment deal, a speaking engagement, or a chance to collaborate on a major project, their network serves as a gateway to new possibilities.

- Learning from Others: Networking allows millionaires to learn from the experiences and expertise of others. By connecting with individuals who have different perspectives, skills, or industry knowledge, millionaires can gain insights that help them make better decisions and avoid costly mistakes.

- Building Trust and Credibility: When millionaires network, they aren't just trying to grow their list of contacts; they're building trust and credibility. Trust is the foundation of any successful relationship, and people are more likely to collaborate, invest, or partner with individuals they trust. By consistently demonstrating integrity, reliability, and competence, millionaires earn the respect and trust of their network.

The Art of Giving Before Receiving

One of the essential principles that millionaires live by is the art of giving before receiving. Rather than approaching networking with a mindset of "what can I get out of this relationship?", they focus on how they can add value to others. This selfless approach builds goodwill, trust, and long-lasting relationships.

Here's how giving before receiving works:

- Offering Help: Millionaires often begin relationships by offering help or valuable insights, whether through sharing knowledge, making introductions, or offering support. By giving first, they demonstrate generosity and a genuine interest in the success of others, which naturally encourages reciprocity in the future.

- Becoming a Connector: Many millionaires act as connectors, helping others in their network by introducing them to people or opportunities that can advance their goals. This creates a web of value, where everyone benefits, and positions the millionaire as a go-to resource within their network.

- Building Long-Term Relationships: Millionaires focus on building long-term, mutually beneficial relationships, rather than short-term transactions. By investing in others without expecting immediate returns, they foster loyalty and trust, which often leads to significant rewards down the road. This approach emphasizes quality over quantity in networking.

Surrounding Oneself with Like-Minded, Ambitious Individuals

The people we spend the most time with have a profound impact on our mindset, habits, and success. Millionaires are keenly aware of this and choose to surround themselves with like-minded, ambitious individuals who share their values and goals. This intentional approach to relationships helps them stay motivated, inspired, and focused on their aspirations.

Here's why surrounding yourself with the right people is critical:

- Elevating Your Standards: Being around driven, successful individuals naturally elevates your standards. High achievers push each other to aim higher, work harder, and continually grow. Millionaires often seek out people who challenge them to be better and hold them accountable for reaching their goals.

- Sharing Knowledge and Resources: Like-minded individuals are more likely to share resources, insights, and strategies that help each other succeed. Whether it's through masterminds, accountability groups, or informal meetings, millionaires create environments where they can learn from others' successes and challenges.

- Positive Influence: Mindset is key to success, and the people you surround yourself with play a significant role in shaping your mindset. Millionaires gravitate toward people who maintain a positive, solutions-oriented outlook on life. This helps them stay optimistic, even in the face of setbacks, and keeps them focused on finding opportunities rather than dwelling on problems.

- Collaborative Opportunities: Ambitious, like-minded individuals often end up collaborating on projects, businesses, or investments. These collaborations are highly valuable because they involve people who share the same work ethic, vision, and commitment to success. By building relationships with such individuals, millionaires create a network of potential partners who can help them achieve their goals.

Building Authentic Relationships

While networking is often associated with business, it's important to note that millionaires value authenticity in their relationships. They don't approach relationships with the sole intent of extracting value; they genuinely care about the people in their network. Authenticity is key to building deep, meaningful connections that stand the test of time.

Here's how millionaires build authentic relationships:

- Listening and Engaging: Millionaires know that strong relationships are built through listening, empathy, and meaningful engagement. They take the time to understand others' goals, challenges, and aspirations, making their interactions more personal and genuine.

- Consistency: Building authentic relationships requires consistency. Millionaires stay in touch with their network regularly, not just when they need something. This could be as simple as checking in, offering congratulations on a milestone, or sharing a relevant resource. Regular communication shows that they value the relationship beyond any potential business transaction.

- Building Trust Through Actions: Trust is the foundation of any relationship, and millionaires build trust through their actions. They follow through on their promises, offer help without expecting anything in return, and consistently demonstrate integrity. Over time, these actions solidify their reputation and strengthen their network.

Leveraging Social Capital

Social capital—the value derived from relationships and networks—is one of the most important assets a millionaire can cultivate. Social capital enables them to access resources, opportunities, and knowledge that they might not have been able to obtain on their own. Millionaires understand that their network is a form of capital, just like financial capital, and they treat it with care and respect.

Here's how millionaires leverage their social capital:

- Expanding Their Reach: Through their network, millionaires gain access to people and resources that can help them achieve their goals. Whether it's meeting potential investors, business partners, or key decision-makers, their social capital allows them to expand their influence and create new opportunities.

- Tapping Into Collective Knowledge: A strong network provides a wealth of knowledge and expertise. Millionaires regularly tap into their network for advice, guidance, and new ideas. They recognize that they don't have to know everything themselves—by leveraging the knowledge and experience of their connections, they can make better decisions and avoid costly mistakes.

- Enhancing Their Reputation: Social capital enhances a millionaire's reputation and credibility. When they are known for being generous, reliable, and trustworthy, people in their network are more likely to recommend them to others, opening up even more opportunities for growth and collaboration.

Examples of Millionaires and Networking

- Richard Branson: The founder of Virgin Group attributes much of his success to his ability to network and build relationships. Branson has always prioritized creating authentic connections with people, and his willingness to listen, offer help, and connect with individuals from all walks of life has contributed significantly to his success.

- Oprah Winfrey: Oprah has built an empire on the foundation of strong relationships. Her genuine interest in people, coupled with her ability to connect with others on an emotional level, has made her one of the most influential people in the world. Through her network, she has created opportunities for collaboration, business ventures, and philanthropy.

- Mark Cuban: The billionaire entrepreneur and investor often emphasizes the importance of networking in building a successful career. Cuban is known for fostering relationships with entrepreneurs and fellow business leaders, using his network to identify investment opportunities, share ideas, and collaborate on projects.

Investing in Your Network

For millionaires, relationships are one of their most valuable assets. They understand that success is not achieved in isolation, but through a network of trusted individuals who support, challenge, and collaborate with them. By giving before receiving, surrounding themselves with ambitious individuals, and building authentic relationships, millionaires create networks that help them achieve their goals.

Learning from networking with successful Entrepreneurs

One of the most powerful aspects of networking, particularly when connecting with successful entrepreneurs from prestigious groups like the Rich 250 list, is the ability to learn directly from those who have already achieved substantial wealth. These individuals have invaluable insights, having navigated the challenges of building businesses, managing investments, and scaling their wealth over time. By networking with these accomplished entrepreneurs, you can gain access to their wealth of knowledge, learn from their mistakes, and adopt the best practices they used to reach their level of success. This form of direct mentorship and exposure to high-level thinking accelerates your learning curve and provides the tools to make more informed decisions on your own wealth-building journey.

For example, by building relationships with entrepreneurs on the Rich 250 list, you gain access to exclusive opportunities that may not be available to the general public. Whether it's investment deals, partnerships, or business ventures, these high-net-worth individuals are often at the forefront of market trends and industry innovations. By aligning yourself with them, you are more likely to hear about and participate in lucrative opportunities early, giving you an advantage in making wealth-accelerating decisions. Many of these successful entrepreneurs are willing to share opportunities within their networks with people they trust and value, which is why cultivating meaningful relationships and maintaining a positive reputation is crucial.

Moreover, networking with successful entrepreneurs fosters an environment where you can exchange ideas and collaborate on ventures, significantly increasing your potential for wealth creation. The connections you make within these circles can lead to strategic partnerships that enhance your business or investment portfolio. Collaborations with individuals from the Rich 250 list often lead to joint ventures that pool resources, knowledge, and influence to create even greater financial success. A well-placed introduction or business referral within this elite network can open doors that would otherwise be difficult or impossible to access, accelerating your wealth-building process exponentially.

Take, for example, the story of Elon Musk, who, through his network of influential entrepreneurs and investors, was able to secure funding and partnerships for his ventures such as Tesla and SpaceX. Musk didn't just rely on his technical knowledge; he used his network to build credibility, gain financial backing, and connect with other innovators. This helped him expand his reach far beyond his initial capabilities, positioning him at the helm of multiple billion-dollar enterprises. Similarly, Richard Branson of the Virgin Group built his empire not only through his own efforts but by leveraging relationships with other successful entrepreneurs who shared his vision of innovation and disruption.

In conclusion, networking with successful entrepreneurs, particularly those on the Rich 250 list, can rapidly increase your wealth by providing you with invaluable insights, exclusive opportunities, and strategic partnerships. The ability to learn from their experiences, gain access to early-stage investments, and collaborate on high-impact ventures significantly enhances your chances of financial success. The more you invest in building and maintaining these connections, the greater your opportunities for wealth acceleration, as your network directly impacts your net worth.

72

CHAPTER 07

FINANCIAL LITERACY AND SMART INVESTING

Financial literacy is the cornerstone of wealth creation. Millionaires understand that in order to build and maintain their wealth, they must be masters of money management. They know how to make their money work for them through smart investing, saving, budgeting, and managing debt. Financial literacy is not just about knowing how to handle cash flow—it's about understanding the principles behind wealth-building and applying them in ways that maximize long-term financial success.

In this chapter, we will explore the principles of financial literacy that millionaires live by. We'll cover the basics of budgeting, saving, investing, and debt management. Then, we'll dive into the different investment strategies that millionaires use to grow their wealth, such as real estate, stocks, and entrepreneurship. We'll also look at how millionaires diversify their portfolios to minimize risk and create multiple streams of income.

The Basics of Financial Literacy

Financial literacy is the ability to understand and effectively use financial skills, such as managing money, budgeting, and investing. Millionaires prioritize financial literacy because they know that without a strong foundation of money management, it's easy to lose wealth just as quickly as it's gained.

Here are the core components of financial literacy:

- Budgeting: Millionaires are disciplined when it comes to budgeting. They create and follow a budget that aligns with their financial goals, ensuring they are living within their means and saving a significant portion of their income. They track their expenses and adjust their spending to prioritize investments, business ventures, or other wealth-building activities.

- Saving: Millionaires understand the importance of saving as a way to create a financial safety net and accumulate capital for future investments. They often follow the principle of "paying yourself first," meaning they set aside savings before spending on non-essential items. Their savings aren't just for emergencies; they also serve as a pool of capital that can be invested to generate more wealth.

- Managing Debt: Millionaires are strategic about debt. They know how to use debt as a tool to leverage opportunities, such as taking out loans to invest in profitable ventures, but they avoid high-interest consumer debt that drains resources. Debt, when used wisely, can be an asset that helps build wealth, but when mismanaged, it becomes a liability that erodes financial security.

- Investing: The most critical aspect of financial literacy for millionaires is understanding how to invest wisely. Millionaires don't just rely on their income from a job or business; they make their money work for them by investing in assets that appreciate in value over time. This brings us to the core of their wealth-building strategy: smart investing.

Smart Investing: Making Money Work for You

Investing is the primary way millionaires grow their wealth. They don't just save money in a bank account with minimal interest; they put their money into investments that generate higher returns over time. Smart investing is about understanding risk, return, and how to balance the two to create a robust portfolio that maximizes long-term growth.

Here are some of the key investment strategies that millionaires use:

- Real Estate: Real estate is one of the most popular investment vehicles for millionaires. Property has the potential to appreciate over time, generate passive rental income, and provide tax advantages. Millionaires invest in real estate as a way to diversify their portfolios and create multiple streams of income. Some focus on residential properties, while others invest in commercial real estate or real estate development projects.

Example: Donald Trump built much of his wealth through real estate investments, starting with residential properties and expanding into commercial real estate. His ability to strategically invest in high-value properties in prime locations contributed significantly to his financial success.

- Stocks and Bonds: Millionaires often invest a portion of their wealth in the stock market, purchasing shares in companies that have the potential for growth. Stocks offer the opportunity for high returns, particularly if the investor chooses companies that experience significant growth over time. Bonds, on the other hand, provide more stable, fixed-income returns and are often used to balance riskier investments like stocks.

Example: Warren Buffett is one of the most famous stock investors in the world. He follows a value investing strategy, focusing on buying stocks of companies he believes are undervalued but have long-term growth potential. His disciplined approach to stock market investing has made him one of the wealthiest individuals in the world.

- Entrepreneurship: Many millionaires either build their wealth through entrepreneurship or invest in other businesses as angel investors or venture capitalists. Entrepreneurship offers unlimited potential for financial growth, as successful businesses can generate significant profits and create substantial returns on investment. For those who don't want to start their own business, investing in startups and small businesses can also provide high returns.

Example: Mark Cuban built his wealth through entrepreneurship, starting with the sale of his company, Broadcast.com, to Yahoo! for billions. He continues to grow his wealth by investing in businesses as an entrepreneur and as a judge on "Shark Tank," where he supports promising startups.

- Private Equity and Hedge Funds: Some millionaires invest in private equity and hedge funds, which are alternative investments typically reserved for high-net-worth individuals. Private equity involves investing in privately held companies, while hedge funds use a range of investment strategies to generate returns. These investments can offer high returns but often come with more risk and require a larger minimum investment.

Diversification: The Key to Managing Risk

One of the most important principles of investing is diversification. Millionaires know that putting all their eggs in one basket is risky, so they spread their investments across different asset classes to reduce risk and increase the potential for returns. Diversification helps protect against market fluctuations in any single asset class, ensuring that even if one investment performs poorly, others may perform well and balance out the losses.

Here's how millionaires diversify their portfolios:

- Multiple Asset Classes: Millionaires invest in a variety of asset classes, such as real estate, stocks, bonds, and commodities. By diversifying across different types of assets, they reduce the risk associated with relying on just one investment. For example, if the stock market experiences a downturn, real estate or bond investments may still generate returns, stabilizing the portfolio.

- Geographic Diversification: Millionaires also diversify geographically by investing in different regions or countries. This protects them from risks associated with political instability, economic downturns, or currency fluctuations in any one country.

- Investment Strategies: To further reduce risk, millionaires use different investment strategies, such as value investing, growth investing, and income investing. This allows them to balance high-risk, high-reward investments with more stable, lower-risk investments that generate consistent income.

Building Passive Income Streams

One of the primary goals of smart investing is to create multiple streams of passive income—money that is earned without requiring active effort, such as rent from real estate properties, dividends from stocks, or interest from bonds. Millionaires focus on building passive income streams because it allows them to generate wealth while freeing up their time to pursue new opportunities.

Here are some common sources of passive income for millionaires:

- Rental Income: Real estate investments can generate rental income, providing a steady stream of cash flow while the property itself appreciates in value.

- Dividends: Many stocks pay dividends, which are regular payments made to shareholders from the company's profits. Dividends provide a consistent income stream without requiring the investor to sell the stock.

- Interest from Bonds: Bonds pay interest to investors, providing a predictable income stream. While bond yields are typically lower than stock returns, they offer more stability and are a key part of a diversified portfolio.

- Business Income: Some millionaires own businesses that generate passive income. For example, they may own a company that is managed by others, allowing them to earn profits without actively running the day-to-day operations.

The Role of Risk Management

Millionaires are not risk-averse, but they are strategic about managing risk. They understand that every investment carries some level of risk, and their goal is to minimize unnecessary risks while maximizing returns. Here's how they manage risk effectively:

- Diversification: As mentioned earlier, diversification is one of the most effective ways to manage risk. By spreading investments across different asset classes, millionaires protect themselves from losing everything in a single downturn.

- Research and Due Diligence: Millionaires don't invest blindly. They conduct thorough research and due diligence before making any investment. This means analyzing financial statements, studying market trends, and seeking advice from trusted advisors.

- Using Debt Wisely: Millionaires use debt strategically to finance investments, but they are careful not to over-leverage themselves. They ensure that the debt they take on can be serviced without putting their financial stability at risk, and they often use debt to invest in appreciating assets rather than liabilities.

Mastering Financial Literacy and Investing

Financial literacy and smart investing are the cornerstones of wealth creation. Millionaires understand how to manage their money effectively, from budgeting and saving to investing in diverse assets that generate long-term returns. By mastering the principles of financial literacy, creating passive income streams, and managing risk, anyone can build a solid financial foundation and grow their wealth.

The fundamentals of smart investing

One of the fundamental principles of smart investing is shaping clear financial goals. Successful millionaires begin by defining specific, measurable, and realistic goals that guide their investment strategies. These goals provide a roadmap, helping investors decide where to allocate resources and how to balance their portfolios. For example, an investor might have long-term goals, such as building wealth for retirement, or short-term goals, like saving for a home purchase. By establishing clear objectives, millionaires create a focus that prevents them from making impulsive decisions based on market fluctuations or short-term economic events. A well-defined financial goal also helps investors stay disciplined, keeping them on track to achieve financial freedom even when challenges arise.

Assessing risk tolerance is another key component of smart investing. Millionaires carefully evaluate how much risk they are willing to take based on their financial goals, age, income, and personal circumstances. This self-awareness enables them to choose investments that align with their risk tolerance, avoiding unnecessary stress or panic when market volatility occurs. Investors with a higher risk tolerance may lean toward aggressive growth strategies like stocks or real estate, while those with a lower tolerance might prefer more conservative options such as bonds or dividend-yielding assets. Understanding risk tolerance ensures that an investor does not overextend themselves financially and helps them build a portfolio that matches their comfort level, providing both stability and growth potential.

Patience is perhaps one of the most overlooked, yet critical, traits in smart investing. Successful millionaires know that building wealth through investments requires a long-term perspective and are willing to wait years, if not decades, for their investments to yield substantial returns. They understand that real wealth is often built slowly over time, through the power of compound interest and the appreciation of assets. By resisting the temptation to chase quick wins or high-risk investments that promise immediate rewards, smart investors focus on consistent, steady growth. They recognize that short-term market corrections or downturns are part of the investment journey and avoid panic selling during volatile periods. Patience allows them to stay committed to their long-term strategies, which often leads to significantly greater returns than trying to time the market.

A key part of this long-term mindset is refraining from decision-making driven by emotions. Emotional investing—buying and selling based on fear, greed, or market hype—can lead to costly mistakes and missed opportunities. For example, during market downturns, an emotionally driven investor might panic and sell their assets at a loss, only to miss out on the subsequent recovery. On the other hand, fear of missing out (FOMO) might lead someone to buy into an overheated market, only for prices to drop shortly after. Millionaires avoid these pitfalls by basing their decisions on solid research, data, and long-term financial plans, rather than reacting impulsively to short-term market movements. They often practice dollar-cost averaging, steadily investing a set amount at regular intervals, which helps smooth out market volatility and eliminates the temptation to time the market emotionally.

In conclusion, the fundamentals of smart investing—shaping clear financial goals, assessing risk tolerance, practicing patience for long-term returns, and avoiding emotionally driven decisions—are essential components of the millionaire mindset. These principles allow successful investors to navigate the complexities of the financial markets with confidence, ensuring steady growth and protection of their wealth over time. By adhering to these tried-and-true practices, anyone can build a solid foundation for financial success.

CHAPTER 08

HEALTH AND WELLBEING

While wealth and success are often associated with financial gain, millionaires understand that their greatest asset is not money—it's their health. Physical and mental well-being are foundational to their ability to perform at high levels, sustain productivity, and make sound decisions. A millionaire's journey toward success is not just about working hard; it's about maintaining the energy, mental clarity, and emotional resilience needed to achieve and enjoy that success.

In this chapter, we will explore the habits that millionaires prioritize to maintain their physical and mental health. From regular exercise to a balanced diet, meditation, and sufficient sleep, these practices help them stay sharp, focused, and creative. We'll also discuss the role of stress management and how adopting a healthy lifestyle is crucial for long-term success.

The Link Between Health and Success

For millionaires, health is not an afterthought—it is a priority. They recognize that their ability to perform at their best is directly linked to their physical and mental health. Poor health can lead to reduced energy levels, impaired decision-making, and increased stress, all of which can hinder productivity and success.

Physical and mental well-being contribute to:

- Sustained Energy: Healthy habits provide the energy necessary to maintain long workdays, tackle challenges, and remain productive.

- Mental Clarity: A well-functioning mind allows for better problem-solving, creativity, and focus, all of which are crucial for decision-making and leadership.

- Emotional Balance: Managing emotions effectively helps millionaires navigate stress, maintain resilience, and build positive relationships in their personal and professional lives.

Exercise: The Power of Physical Activity

Regular physical activity is one of the most common habits shared by millionaires. Exercise not only improves physical health but also boosts mental health by releasing endorphins, which are chemicals in the brain that reduce stress and enhance mood. Whether it's running, swimming, weightlifting, yoga, or cycling, millionaires make time for exercise because they know it has a profound impact on their overall well-being.

Here's how regular exercise contributes to success:

- Increased Energy Levels: Physical activity boosts energy by improving cardiovascular health and increasing stamina. Millionaires who exercise regularly have more energy throughout the day, allowing them to tackle challenges with vigor and focus.

- Improved Mental Health: Exercise reduces symptoms of anxiety, depression, and stress, providing a natural way to manage the emotional challenges that come with a high-pressure lifestyle. Millionaires often use exercise as a way to clear their minds and reduce mental clutter.

- Enhanced Focus and Productivity: Exercise improves cognitive function, enhancing memory, attention, and problem-solving abilities. Many successful individuals report that regular physical activity helps them stay focused and productive throughout the day.

Balanced Diet: Fueling the Body and Mind

What we put into our bodies directly affects how we perform, both physically and mentally. Millionaires understand the importance of a balanced diet, which provides the nutrients needed to sustain energy levels, improve cognitive function, and support long-term health. Rather than relying on fast food or processed meals, they prioritize whole, nutrient-rich foods that fuel their bodies and minds.

Here are some common dietary habits of millionaires:

- Eating Whole Foods: Millionaires focus on whole, unprocessed foods like vegetables, fruits, lean proteins, and healthy fats. These foods provide essential nutrients that support brain health, boost energy, and prevent chronic diseases.

- Limiting Sugar and Processed Foods: Processed foods, especially those high in sugar, can lead to energy crashes and cognitive fog. Millionaires avoid these foods to maintain consistent energy levels and mental clarity throughout the day.

- Staying Hydrated: Proper hydration is key to maintaining focus and cognitive function. Many millionaires prioritize drinking water throughout the day, recognizing that dehydration can impair mental and physical performance.

A healthy diet is not about restriction; it's about providing the body with the fuel it needs to function optimally. Millionaires who prioritize nutrition find that they have more energy, sharper focus, and greater resilience against illness and fatigue.

Meditation and Mindfulness: Mental Clarity and Emotional Balance

Mental clarity and emotional balance are just as important as physical health when it comes to success. Many millionaires incorporate mindfulness practices like meditation into their daily routines as a way to manage stress, improve focus, and cultivate a sense of calm. Meditation helps them clear their minds, gain perspective, and approach challenges with a level-headed mindset.

Here's why meditation is a powerful tool for success:

- Reducing Stress: Meditation activates the parasympathetic nervous system, which helps calm the body and reduce stress. Millionaires use meditation to lower cortisol levels, allowing them to manage the demands of their work and personal lives more effectively.

- Improved Focus and Decision-Making: Meditation sharpens focus by training the mind to stay present and avoid distractions. This heightened sense of awareness improves decision-making, as millionaires can approach problems with a clear and focused mindset.

- Emotional Intelligence: Meditation fosters emotional intelligence by helping individuals become more aware of their emotions and how they react to stress. Millionaires who meditate are better equipped to handle pressure, manage relationships, and navigate the ups and downs of life.

Sufficient Sleep: The Foundation of Health

Sleep is often overlooked in discussions about success, but it is one of the most critical components of health and well-being. Millionaires prioritize sleep because they understand that inadequate rest impairs cognitive function, weakens the immune system, and leads to burnout. They know that sleep is not a luxury—it's a necessity.

Here's why sleep is essential for success:

- Cognitive Function: Sleep plays a vital role in memory, learning, and problem-solving. Millionaires who prioritize sleep find that they are more alert, focused, and creative when they are well-rested.

- Emotional Resilience: Lack of sleep can lead to mood swings, irritability, and poor emotional regulation. Millionaires who get sufficient rest are better able to handle stress, maintain positive relationships, and stay emotionally balanced.

- Physical Health: Sleep is crucial for maintaining a healthy immune system and preventing chronic conditions like heart disease, diabetes, and obesity. By getting enough rest, millionaires protect their long-term health and ensure they have the energy to pursue their goals.

Successful individuals typically aim for 7-9 hours of sleep per night, knowing that consistent, quality rest is essential for peak performance.

Stress Management: Thriving Under Pressure

The lives of millionaires are often filled with high-pressure situations, but they know how to manage stress effectively. Chronic stress can lead to burnout, reduced productivity, and health problems, so millionaires make it a point to develop habits that reduce stress and promote well-being.

Here are some of the ways millionaires manage stress:

- Delegation: Millionaires are skilled at delegating tasks to trusted team members, which allows them to focus on the most important aspects of their business without becoming overwhelmed by details.

- Time Management: Effective time management reduces stress by allowing millionaires to prioritize tasks and avoid feeling overwhelmed by their workload. They often use time-blocking, to-do lists, and goal-setting to stay organized and on top of their responsibilities.

- Engaging in Hobbies: Millionaires often have hobbies that help them unwind and recharge. Whether it's playing a sport, spending time in nature, or pursuing a creative passion, engaging in enjoyable activities is a crucial part of their stress management strategy.

A Holistic Approach to Health and Wellbeing

Millionaires take a holistic approach to health and well-being. They understand that physical, mental, and emotional health are interconnected, and they prioritize practices that support all three areas. By maintaining balance in their lives, they are able to perform at high levels without sacrificing their health or happiness.

Examples of Millionaires Who Prioritize Health

- Richard Branson: The founder of the Virgin Group is known for his commitment to health and fitness. Branson starts his day with exercise, whether it's kite surfing, tennis, or cycling, and he credits his active lifestyle with giving him the energy to manage his businesses and personal ventures.

- Arianna Huffington: The co-founder of The Huffington Post is a vocal advocate for sleep and well-being. After experiencing burnout herself, Huffington wrote the book The Sleep Revolution, which highlights the importance of sleep in achieving success.

- Tony Robbins: The world-renowned motivational speaker and entrepreneur is a strong proponent of physical and mental health. Robbins incorporates exercise, a healthy diet, and meditation into his daily routine to maintain his high energy levels and mental clarity.

Health as a Foundation for Success

For millionaires, health is not something to be taken for granted—it's a non-negotiable aspect of their success. By prioritizing regular exercise, a balanced diet, meditation, sufficient sleep, and stress management, they maintain the physical and mental well-being necessary to achieve and sustain their goals. Health and success go hand in hand, and without a strong foundation of well-being, long-term success is impossible.

The positive correlation between wealth and health

There is a clear and positive correlation between wealth and health, which plays a significant role in the lives of millionaires. Wealthier individuals often have access to better living conditions, such as safer neighborhoods, access to nutritious food, and cleaner environments. These living conditions create a foundation for maintaining physical health and reducing the risk of certain diseases. For example, wealthier individuals can afford fresh, organic food, exercise equipment, gym memberships, and healthcare services, all of which contribute to overall wellbeing. In contrast, people with fewer financial resources may have limited access to healthy food and may live in environments with higher pollution or unsafe conditions, which can negatively impact their health over time.

One of the most significant benefits of wealth is the ability to maintain lower levels of stress, which directly contributes to better mental and physical health. Financial stability reduces anxiety related to day-to-day survival, such as worrying about paying bills or facing unexpected expenses. Millionaires, who generally experience less financial pressure, can focus on long-term planning rather than managing financial crises. This lower stress level is crucial because chronic stress is linked to numerous health problems, including heart disease, diabetes, and mental health disorders such as anxiety and depression. By having the financial means to manage life's demands more easily, wealthier individuals often experience less of the constant strain that comes with financial uncertainty.

Additionally, wealth is associated with fewer chronic health conditions and longer life expectancy. Millionaires are more likely to invest in preventive healthcare, such as regular medical checkups, early detection screenings, and top-tier health services that can detect and treat issues before they become serious. They have access to advanced medical treatments and specialists, enabling them to manage and recover from health problems more effectively. For example, high-net-worth individuals are often able to afford concierge healthcare services, which provide more personalized and immediate medical attention. This proactive approach to health enables them to live longer, healthier lives, free from the chronic illnesses that often plague individuals with limited access to healthcare.

In conclusion, the correlation between wealth and health is undeniable. Wealthier people not only enjoy better living conditions and reduced stress but also have the financial resources to invest in preventative healthcare and live healthier, longer lives. By prioritizing health and wellbeing, millionaires are able to maintain the energy, focus, and longevity necessary to continue building and preserving their wealth.

CHAPTER 09

GENEROSITY AND GIVING BACK

For many millionaires, wealth is not just about personal gain—it's also about making a positive impact on the world. One of the most rewarding aspects of their success is the ability to give back to their communities and contribute to causes that matter to them. Philanthropy and generosity play significant roles in the lives of millionaires, offering them a sense of purpose and fulfillment beyond financial achievement.

In this chapter, we will explore how millionaires incorporate giving back into their lives, and the different forms that generosity can take. From charitable donations to mentoring and community service, we will see how giving back not only benefits society but also enhances the personal and emotional well-being of those who give. For many successful individuals, philanthropy is a way to leave a legacy and create lasting change.

The Power of Purpose and Fulfillment

Many millionaires reach a point in their financial journey where accumulating wealth is no longer their primary focus. Instead, they begin to seek a greater sense of purpose and fulfillment, often turning to philanthropy as a way to make a meaningful difference. While financial success brings its own rewards, millionaires often find deeper satisfaction in knowing that their wealth can improve the lives of others.

Generosity helps millionaires:

- Create a Legacy: Philanthropy allows millionaires to leave a lasting legacy by supporting causes they are passionate about. Whether it's funding education, healthcare, or environmental initiatives, their contributions can create positive change that extends beyond their lifetime.

- Gain a Sense of Purpose: Giving back provides millionaires with a sense of purpose, helping them connect their wealth to something greater than themselves. Knowing that they are making a difference in the world gives them motivation and fulfillment.

- Inspire Others: Millionaires who lead by example in giving back often inspire others to do the same. Their philanthropy can spark a ripple effect, encouraging their peers, employees, and communities to become more involved in charitable efforts.

Philanthropy: Charitable Donations

One of the most common ways millionaires give back is through charitable donations. Many successful individuals establish foundations, donate to non-profit organizations, or contribute directly to causes they care about. Charitable giving allows them to leverage their wealth to address societal challenges and support the work of organizations that are making a positive impact.

Here are some common areas where millionaires direct their philanthropic efforts:

- Education: Many millionaires choose to support education, recognizing it as a critical tool for lifting people out of poverty and creating opportunities for future generations. They may fund scholarships, build schools, or contribute to educational programs that provide access to quality learning.

Example: Bill and Melinda Gates have directed billions of dollars toward improving global education through their foundation, particularly focusing on initiatives that increase access to education in underserved communities.

- Healthcare: Healthcare is another area where philanthropy can make a significant difference. Millionaires often contribute to medical research, hospitals, and public health programs to improve access to healthcare and fund advancements in medical treatments.

Example: Michael Bloomberg has donated billions to public health causes, including anti-smoking campaigns, COVID-19 response efforts, and initiatives to address health inequities around the world.

- Environmental Conservation: Environmental causes, such as climate change, wildlife preservation, and sustainability efforts, are important to many millionaires. Through charitable donations, they help fund research, conservation programs, and policies that protect the planet for future generations.

Example: Elon Musk has pledged significant contributions to initiatives aimed at addressing climate change and promoting sustainability, particularly through his work with Tesla and SpaceX.

- Social Justice: Some millionaires focus on social justice causes, supporting initiatives that address inequality, discrimination, and systemic injustice. These donations often fund programs that empower marginalized communities and advocate for human rights.

Example: Oprah Winfrey has long been an advocate for social justice and has made substantial donations to causes that promote racial equality, gender equality, and access to education for disadvantaged communities.

Mentoring and Coaching

Beyond financial donations, many millionaires give back by sharing their knowledge and experience with others. Mentoring is a powerful way for successful individuals to pass on their expertise, providing guidance and support to aspiring entrepreneurs, young professionals, and those looking to advance in their careers.

Mentoring offers several key benefits:

- Empowering Others: By offering mentorship, millionaires empower others to achieve their goals and overcome challenges. They can provide insights into business, leadership, and personal development that help their mentees navigate complex situations.

- Creating Opportunities: Mentors often help open doors for their mentees by introducing them to valuable networks, providing career advice, or offering business opportunities. Millionaires who mentor others are often able to help their mentees unlock new opportunities that might have been difficult to access otherwise.

- Passing on Values: Mentorship allows millionaires to pass on not only their technical expertise but also the values that have guided their success. They can inspire a new generation of leaders to adopt principles of integrity, perseverance, and service.

Example: Richard Branson, the founder of Virgin Group, is known for his commitment to mentoring young entrepreneurs. He frequently shares his experiences and advice through public speaking, writing, and direct mentorship, helping others build successful businesses.

Community Service and Volunteerism

Community service and volunteerism are also important ways millionaires give back. While financial donations are impactful, many successful individuals also dedicate their time and skills to supporting causes they care about. This hands-on approach allows them to connect with the people and communities they are helping on a deeper level.

Here's how millionaires engage in community service:

- Volunteering: Some millionaires choose to volunteer their time to non-profit organizations or community initiatives. Whether it's serving meals at a homeless shelter, participating in environmental cleanups, or providing pro-bono services, volunteering allows them to make a direct impact.

- Leading Community Initiatives: Many successful individuals take on leadership roles in community service, organizing events, fundraising efforts, or campaigns that bring attention to important causes. By leveraging their influence, they can mobilize others to get involved and contribute to their community.

Example: LeBron James has made significant contributions to his hometown of Akron, Ohio, through community service initiatives, including the establishment of the LeBron James Family Foundation, which focuses on improving education for underserved students.

Social Entrepreneurship

Another way millionaires give back is through social entrepreneurship—using business as a tool to address social or environmental issues. Rather than focusing solely on profits, social entrepreneurs create businesses that aim to make a positive impact on the world while still being financially sustainable.

Social entrepreneurship allows millionaires to:

- Combine Profit with Purpose: Social entrepreneurs create businesses that tackle societal challenges while generating revenue. By aligning their business goals with social good, they create sustainable solutions that benefit both shareholders and society.

- Drive Innovation for Social Impact: Many social entrepreneurs focus on innovative solutions to global problems, such as clean energy, access to clean water, or affordable healthcare. These businesses not only generate wealth but also contribute to solving pressing issues facing the world.

Example: Blake Mycoskie, the founder of TOMS Shoes, pioneered the "one-for-one" model, where for every pair of shoes sold, the company donates a pair to a person in need. This approach has had a significant impact on global poverty while creating a successful business.

The Ripple Effect of Generosity

Generosity is not just about the immediate impact of a donation or act of service—it creates a ripple effect that can inspire others to give back. Millionaires who lead by example in their philanthropic efforts often encourage those around them to adopt a mindset of giving. Whether it's their employees, peers, or family members, their generosity sets a standard that influences others to contribute to the causes they care about.

This ripple effect of generosity extends beyond individual contributions, creating a culture of giving that can lead to broader social change.

The Emotional Benefits of Giving Back

While the primary goal of philanthropy is to make a positive impact, giving back also has emotional benefits for those who give. Millionaires often find that generosity enhances their own sense of happiness, purpose, and fulfillment. Research shows that acts of giving—whether through financial donations, time, or skills—can improve emotional well-being, reduce stress, and increase feelings of connectedness.

For many successful individuals, the emotional rewards of giving back are just as significant as the financial rewards of their careers. Knowing that they are contributing to a better world provides a sense of meaning and satisfaction that wealth alone cannot offer.

The Role of Generosity in Success

Generosity and giving back are integral parts of a millionaire's journey. Whether through charitable donations, mentoring, community service, or social entrepreneurship, successful individuals use their wealth and influence to create positive change in the world. For millionaires, the ability to give back is not just a byproduct of their success—it is a source of purpose, fulfillment, and lasting impact.

Why many Millionaires are generous with their wealth?

Many millionaires are generous with their wealth, and this generosity is often rooted in a deep sense of responsibility and purpose. Having achieved financial success, many feel compelled to use their wealth to positively impact the world around them. This drive to give back is not only a reflection of their gratitude but also a recognition that their success is, in part, a result of the opportunities, support, and communities that shaped them. For many, philanthropy becomes a way to create lasting change, whether through funding educational programs, healthcare initiatives, or social causes. By contributing to society, millionaires often experience a sense of fulfillment that transcends personal wealth, knowing that their resources are helping others thrive.

One common reason why millionaires are generous is the belief in the principle of "paying it forward". Many self-made millionaires understand the struggles of starting from the bottom and have experienced the impact that mentorship, financial support, or opportunity can have on an individual's life. For them, giving back is a way to offer others the same chances that they had or lacked. This often takes the form of mentoring young entrepreneurs, funding scholarships, or investing in community development projects. These actions not only help others build their own paths to success but also reinforce the millionaire's legacy of fostering growth and innovation. Furthermore, by sharing their wealth and knowledge, they contribute to creating a more sustainable and prosperous society.

There are many ways that millionaires give back, reflecting their diverse interests and values. Some choose charitable donations to specific causes, such as education, healthcare, or poverty alleviation, while others establish foundations to manage their philanthropy on a larger scale, ensuring that their wealth continues to fund important causes for generations. Others prefer to give through impact investing, where they invest in businesses and projects that generate social or environmental benefits alongside financial returns. For example, tech billionaires like Bill Gates have dedicated significant portions of their fortunes to global health and education initiatives through the Bill & Melinda Gates Foundation. Additionally, many millionaires give back through community service, offering their time and expertise to nonprofit organizations, or by creating initiatives that address pressing social challenges, such as climate change or inequality.

Generosity is not just an occasional act for many millionaires but a core value that drives their approach to wealth. This mindset often transforms how they view their financial success, shifting the focus from accumulation to distribution and legacy-building. By choosing to use their resources for the greater good, millionaires align their wealth with a sense of social impact, which not only enhances their personal satisfaction but also reinforces their standing in the business and social worlds. In many cases, their philanthropy serves as an extension of their vision, allowing them to influence societal progress long after their business ventures have matured or ended. This enduring contribution to the world becomes a defining aspect of their success, showcasing how wealth, when used with intention, can create long-term benefits for humanity.

Moreover, philanthropy often opens doors for millionaires to collaborate with other high-impact individuals and organizations. These partnerships amplify their ability to effect change on a larger scale. By pooling their resources, they can tackle bigger issues, such as global poverty, environmental sustainability, or medical research. These collaborative efforts are evident in initiatives like the Giving Pledge, where billionaires commit to donating the majority of their wealth to charitable causes, or in impact-driven networks that address systemic global challenges. For instance, Warren Buffett's pledge to donate most of his wealth to charity has inspired other wealthy individuals to think more broadly about the role their wealth can play in reshaping society for the better. This collective approach to giving multiplies the effects of individual efforts and establishes a legacy of generosity that stretches beyond personal gain.

Additionally, millionaires understand that generosity often creates reciprocal benefits. While their giving may be altruistic, it also fosters goodwill, strengthens relationships, and can open up new opportunities for growth, both personally and professionally. Many wealthy individuals find that by contributing to the welfare of others, they build networks that extend beyond business, entering realms of influence that can generate new ventures, innovations, or insights. The respect and recognition that comes with their philanthropy often circles back to them in the form of deeper connections, greater influence, and enhanced social capital. This cycle of giving and receiving helps sustain their personal growth and prosperity, illustrating how generosity is not just about financial transactions but about building an ecosystem where wealth, wisdom, and influence circulate to benefit everyone involved.

In summary, millionaires embrace generosity as a core element of their success, using their wealth to impact the world positively. Whether through direct charitable donations, collaborative initiatives, or personal mentoring, their generosity becomes a means of creating lasting value, reinforcing their legacy, and connecting them to broader networks of influence and opportunity. This deep commitment to giving not only shapes their identities but also multiplies the impact of their wealth, demonstrating that the true measure of success often lies in how much one gives back.

CHAPTER 10

THE POWER OF PERSISTENCE

One of the most essential traits that millionaires possess is persistence. While talent, intelligence, and opportunity play significant roles in achieving success, it is persistence—the ability to continue pursuing goals despite obstacles—that ultimately sets successful individuals apart. Millionaires understand that the road to success is rarely smooth and that setbacks are inevitable. However, it is their refusal to give up in the face of adversity that allows them to push forward and reach their financial and personal goals.

In this chapter, we will explore the power of persistence and share stories of millionaires who overcame significant challenges on their path to success. We'll examine how perseverance, patience, and maintaining a positive attitude are critical to navigating setbacks and achieving long-term goals.

The Role of Persistence in Success

Persistence is the ability to keep going when things get tough. It's easy to stay motivated when everything is going well, but the true test of one's character comes during times of hardship. Millionaires understand that success is not about avoiding obstacles; it's about learning how to overcome them and continuing to move forward.

Here's why persistence is crucial for success:

- Turning Failures into Lessons: Every successful millionaire has experienced failure at some point. However, rather than seeing failure as a defeat, they view it as an opportunity to learn and grow. Persistence means pushing through failure, analyzing what went wrong, and using that knowledge to improve.

- The Long-Term Vision: Millionaires often have big dreams that take years, if not decades, to achieve. Persistence is what keeps them focused on their long-term vision, even when progress seems slow or when immediate results are lacking. They understand that success is a marathon, not a sprint, and that patience is required to reach their goals.

- Building Mental Resilience: Every challenge or setback faced along the way helps build mental resilience.

Persistence requires mental toughness—the ability to stay focused, maintain confidence, and keep going even when it feels like the odds are stacked against you.

Stories of Persistence: Millionaires Who Overcame Obstacles

Every millionaire has a story of persistence—a time when they faced a significant challenge but refused to give up. Let's look at a few examples of individuals who exemplified persistence and ultimately achieved remarkable success.

1. J.K. Rowling

The author of the Harry Potter series, J.K. Rowling, is one of the most inspiring examples of persistence. Before achieving global fame, Rowling faced numerous challenges. As a single mother living on government assistance, she struggled to make ends meet. When she finished the manuscript for Harry Potter and the Philosopher's Stone, it was rejected by 12 publishers. Despite these rejections, Rowling refused to give up on her dream of becoming an author. Her persistence eventually paid off when a small publisher took a chance on her manuscript, leading to one of the most successful book franchises in history.

2. Howard Schultz

Howard Schultz, the former CEO of Starbucks, grew up in a poor family and faced significant obstacles on his journey to success. When he initially approached investors to expand Starbucks, he was rejected over 200 times. Despite the numerous rejections, Schultz believed in his vision and continued to pursue his goal. His persistence led him to build Starbucks into a global brand, transforming the way the world experiences coffee.

3. Oprah Winfrey

Oprah Winfrey's rise to success is a powerful example of perseverance in the face of adversity. Born into poverty and facing numerous personal challenges throughout her childhood, Winfrey overcame immense obstacles to pursue a career in broadcasting. Early in her career, she faced setbacks, including being demoted from her first television job. However, she refused to let these challenges define her. Through persistence, she eventually became one of the most successful media moguls in history, with a career spanning television, publishing, and philanthropy.

The Importance of Patience and Delayed Gratification

One of the key elements of persistence is patience. Millionaires understand that success rarely happens overnight. They are willing to delay gratification, focusing on long-term goals rather than seeking immediate rewards. This ability to stay committed to the process, even when results are not yet visible, is what sets persistent individuals apart from those who give up too soon.

Here's why patience is essential to persistence:

- Building Momentum: Success often requires sustained effort over an extended period. Millionaires know that it takes time to build momentum, whether they're growing a business, investing, or pursuing personal development. They stay patient, trusting that their hard work will eventually pay off.

- Avoiding Burnout: Patience helps prevent burnout. Millionaires pace themselves, understanding that taking on too much too quickly can lead to exhaustion. By setting realistic expectations and breaking down their goals into manageable steps, they maintain their energy and motivation over the long haul.

- Recognizing Progress: Persistence requires celebrating small wins along the way. Millionaires understand that every small step forward is progress, even if it doesn't lead to immediate success. This perspective allows them to remain positive and motivated, even during slow periods.

Maintaining a Positive Attitude in the Face of Challenges

Maintaining a positive attitude is a crucial part of persistence. Millionaires who are persistent understand that setbacks and failures are not the end—they are simply part of the journey. By staying optimistic and keeping a solution-focused mindset, they are better able to navigate challenges and keep moving forward.

Here's how maintaining a positive attitude supports persistence:

- Reframing Challenges: Millionaires often view challenges as opportunities for growth rather than as roadblocks. By reframing difficulties as learning experiences, they are able to maintain a positive mindset and continue working toward their goals.

- Staying Motivated: A positive attitude helps millionaires stay motivated, even when the going gets tough. They focus on the progress they've made rather than dwelling on setbacks, allowing them to maintain momentum and avoid getting discouraged.

- Attracting Opportunities: Optimism and persistence tend to attract opportunities. People who maintain a positive attitude are more likely to take calculated risks, pursue new ventures, and surround themselves with supportive individuals who can help them succeed.

Learning from Setbacks

Setbacks are inevitable on the path to success, but millionaires understand that each setback is an opportunity to learn and grow. Rather than being discouraged by failure, they use setbacks as valuable feedback that helps them refine their approach. This mindset of continuous improvement is key to persistence.

Here's how millionaires learn from setbacks:

- Analyzing Mistakes: When faced with failure, millionaires take the time to analyze what went wrong. They look at their strategies, decisions, and actions to identify areas where they can improve. This willingness to learn from mistakes allows them to adjust their course and avoid making the same errors in the future.

- Adapting and Evolving: Persistence doesn't mean sticking to a plan that isn't working—it means being adaptable and open to change. Millionaires are willing to pivot when necessary, adjusting their strategies to better align with their goals. By staying flexible, they ensure that their persistence leads to progress, not stagnation.

- Developing Resilience: Setbacks help millionaires build resilience—the ability to recover quickly from difficulties. Each time they overcome a challenge, they become stronger and more confident in their ability to navigate future obstacles.

The Compound Effect of Persistence

Persistence is not just about enduring difficult times; it's about consistently taking action over the long term. The compound effect refers to the idea that small, consistent actions accumulate over time to create massive results. Millionaires understand that by staying persistent and taking action day after day, they are building momentum that will eventually lead to success.

Here's why the compound effect is so powerful:

- Small Steps Lead to Big Results: Persistence is about making incremental progress. Millionaires focus on taking small, consistent steps toward their goals, trusting that over time, these efforts will add up to significant achievements.

- Consistency Builds Confidence: Each time millionaires take action, they build confidence in their abilities. This confidence reinforces their persistence, creating a positive feedback loop that keeps them motivated and moving forward.

- Momentum Fuels Success: As millionaires stay persistent, they build momentum. This momentum makes it easier to keep going, even when challenges arise. Over time, their persistence leads to a tipping point where success becomes inevitable.

Persistence as the Key to Long-Term Success

Persistence is the key to unlocking long-term success. Millionaires who achieve greatness do so not because they never face challenges, but because they refuse to give up when challenges arise. By maintaining a positive attitude, practicing patience, and learning from setbacks, they are able to overcome obstacles and continue moving toward their goals.

For anyone aspiring to achieve financial success or personal fulfillment, persistence is non-negotiable. It is the trait that will carry you through difficult times, help you learn from failures, and ultimately lead to the realization of your dreams.

As we conclude this book, remember that the habits and traits of millionaires—vision, discipline, learning, adaptability, resilience, networking, smart investing, health, generosity, and persistence—are accessible to anyone willing to adopt them. By applying these principles consistently, you can create a path to your own version of success.

How to Stop Quitting on Yourself and Achieve Your Goals

One of the most common obstacles people face on their journey to success is quitting on themselves before they reach their goals. Millionaires, however, have mastered the art of persistence and have developed the mental resilience to stay the course even when the road becomes difficult. The key to stopping the habit of quitting on yourself lies in understanding that setbacks and challenges are part of the process, not indicators of failure. By shifting your mindset to view obstacles as learning opportunities, you can cultivate the determination needed to push through moments of doubt and frustration.

One effective way to stop quitting is to break your larger goals into smaller, more manageable milestones. This approach makes the journey less overwhelming and provides frequent wins to keep you motivated. For example, if your goal is to build a successful business, rather than focusing solely on the end result of profitability, break it down into actionable steps such as acquiring your first clients, developing a marketing strategy, or launching a product. Each of these smaller victories builds momentum and reinforces your belief in your ability to succeed. Additionally, having a clear "why"—a deep, personal reason for pursuing your goals—can help you stay focused when external motivation wanes. When you connect your goals to a meaningful purpose, it becomes harder to give up, as the stakes are higher than just personal achievement.

Persistence also involves mastering the art of self-discipline, which means doing what needs to be done, even when you don't feel like it. Millionaires succeed because they understand that motivation can be fleeting, but discipline is constant. To cultivate discipline, you need to establish habits that align with your goals. Create a daily routine that prioritizes consistent progress, even in small increments. This could include setting aside specific times for working on your goals, removing distractions, or developing systems for accountability, such as sharing your progress with a mentor or a trusted friend. Over time, these small actions compound, and before you know it, you've achieved significant milestones simply by showing up consistently.

Stopping the cycle of quitting on yourself and achieving your goals requires a commitment to persistence, a shift in mindset, and the establishment of disciplined routines. By breaking down large goals into smaller tasks, focusing on your personal "why," and developing a system of consistent habits, you can stay the course even when challenges arise. The power of persistence ensures that, regardless of the obstacles you face, you keep moving forward, turning setbacks into stepping stones toward your ultimate success.

Another critical factor in breaking the habit of quitting is learning to embrace failure as part of the journey rather than a signal to stop. Millionaires understand that failure is not the opposite of success but a necessary step toward it. When you view failure as a teacher, you gain valuable insights that can propel you forward with better strategies and stronger resolve. Instead of fearing setbacks, you should train yourself to expect them and even welcome them as an opportunity for growth. Each time you stumble or fall short of a goal, ask yourself, "What can I learn from this?" This reflection helps you refine your approach, ensuring that each failure moves you closer to success rather than away from it.

One of the key qualities that set successful individuals apart is their ability to persevere through adversity. When faced with obstacles, they don't quit; instead, they find ways to adapt and pivot. Take the story of Thomas Edison, who famously failed over a thousand times before inventing the lightbulb. When asked about his repeated failures, he said, "I have not failed. I've just found 10,000 ways that won't work." Edison's ability to persist despite countless setbacks is a prime example of how a resilient mindset can lead to world-changing innovations. Adopting a similar attitude—seeing each challenge as a stepping stone—allows you to build the mental toughness needed to persevere, even when the road seems impossible.

Lastly, to stop quitting on yourself, you must surround yourself with positive influences. Your environment plays a significant role in shaping your mindset and, by extension, your ability to persist. If you are surrounded by people who encourage you, hold you accountable, and believe in your vision, you are far less likely to give up when challenges arise. Millionaires often credit their success to being part of a network that supports and uplifts them. Whether it's mentors, peers, or coaches, having the right people around you creates a buffer against self-doubt and discouragement. Seek out individuals who inspire and challenge you to keep pushing forward, and avoid those who sow seeds of negativity or doubt. Building a strong support system ensures that when you feel like quitting, there's someone to remind you of your capabilities and keep you on track.

In conclusion, the power of persistence lies in embracing failure, adapting to setbacks, and cultivating a positive environment that supports your goals. Millionaires are not immune to difficulties or doubt, but what makes them successful is their unwavering commitment to keep going. By shifting your mindset, learning from failures, and surrounding yourself with the right influences, you can develop the resilience to stop quitting on yourself and achieve the success you seek.

CONCLUSION

APPLYING MILLIONAIRE HABITS TO YOUR LIFE

As we conclude this exploration of the habits and traits that set millionaires apart, it's clear that financial success is not a matter of luck or privilege. Rather, it is the result of intentional, disciplined actions practiced consistently over time. Millionaires aren't simply born into wealth; many achieve it by adopting mindsets and behaviors that allow them to overcome obstacles, build wealth, and live purpose-driven lives. The good news is that these habits can be adopted by anyone who is willing to commit to growth, discipline, and persistence.

In this final chapter, we will summarize the key takeaways from this book and provide practical steps you can take to start incorporating millionaire habits into your own life. The journey to financial success begins with mindset, but it's sustained by consistent actions and a dedication to continuous improvement.

Key Takeaways from the Book

Throughout this book, we've identified several key habits and traits that contribute to the success of millionaires:

1. Vision and Goal Setting: Millionaires think long-term and set specific, measurable goals that guide their decisions and actions. By creating a clear vision and establishing a roadmap to achieve it, they stay focused and motivated, even when challenges arise.

2. Discipline and Consistency: Success requires discipline—the ability to stick to plans and routines, even when motivation fades. Millionaires consistently take action, maintain productive habits, and stay disciplined in their pursuit of long-term goals.

3. Continuous Learning: Millionaires are lifelong learners, constantly seeking new knowledge and skills. Whether through reading, attending seminars, or networking with others, they understand that continuous learning is essential for staying competitive and innovative.

4. Risk-Taking and Decision Making: Successful individuals take calculated risks and make informed decisions. They don't shy away from uncertainty but approach risks with a strategic mindset, knowing that growth often requires stepping out of their comfort zones.

5. Resilience and Adaptability: In the face of setbacks, millionaires demonstrate remarkable resilience. They adapt to changing circumstances and use adversity as a stepping stone to greater success. Mental toughness and emotional intelligence help them stay focused on their goals.

6. Networking and Relationships: Millionaires build strong networks and surround themselves with like-minded, ambitious individuals. They understand the value of giving before receiving and leverage their relationships to create opportunities and grow their influence.

7. Financial Literacy and Smart Investing: Millionaires know how to manage money wisely, budget effectively, and invest in ways that make their money work for them. They diversify their investments and focus on long-term financial growth through real estate, stocks, and entrepreneurship.

8. Health and Wellbeing: Physical and mental health are foundational to sustained success. Millionaires prioritize exercise, a balanced diet, sufficient sleep, and stress management to maintain their energy, focus, and creativity.

9. Generosity and Giving Back: Millionaires believe in using their wealth and influence to make a positive impact. Through charitable donations, mentorship, and community service, they create a legacy of generosity and inspire others to give back.

10. Persistence: Perhaps the most important trait of all, persistence is what carries millionaires through challenges and setbacks. By staying focused on their goals, maintaining a positive attitude, and refusing to give up, they achieve long-term success.

Practical Steps to Adopt Millionaire Habits

While the journey to financial success may seem daunting, it is entirely achievable by taking small, consistent steps in the right direction. Here are some practical ways to start applying millionaire habits to your life:

1. Define Your Vision and Set Goals: Take time to clarify your long-term vision. What do you want to achieve financially, professionally, and personally? Once you have a clear vision, set SMART goals (specific, measurable, attainable, relevant, and time-bound) to help you move toward that vision. Break your goals into smaller, actionable steps that you can work on each day.

2. Develop a Daily Routine: Establish a daily routine that aligns with your goals. This could include waking up early, setting aside time for exercise, dedicating focused hours to work or learning, and practicing mindfulness or meditation. Consistency is key, so commit to following your routine even when motivation dips.

3. Invest in Your Education: Make continuous learning a priority. Set aside time each day or week to read

books, take courses, or attend seminars related to your field or personal interests. Seek out mentors or join networking groups where you can learn from others and share your experiences.

4. Take Calculated Risks: Don't be afraid to step out of your comfort zone. Whether it's starting a new business, investing in a new opportunity, or making a career change, assess the risks and rewards, then make informed decisions. Remember, growth often requires taking bold but calculated steps.

5. Build Resilience: Practice mental and emotional resilience by reframing challenges as opportunities for growth. When faced with setbacks, reflect on what you can learn from the experience and adjust your approach. Develop healthy coping mechanisms for stress, such as exercise, meditation, or spending time with loved ones.

6. Surround Yourself with Positive, Ambitious People: Evaluate the people you spend the most time with. Are they supportive, ambitious, and positive? If not, consider seeking out new relationships with like-minded individuals who inspire and challenge you. Build your network by attending events, joining professional groups, or reaching out to potential mentors.

7. Master Your Finances: Take control of your finances by creating a budget, saving a portion of your income, and learning about smart investing. Start small, but be consistent in building your wealth through disciplined financial habits. Consider diversifying your investments to minimize risk and generate long-term returns.

8. Prioritize Health and Wellbeing: Commit to taking care of your body and mind. Schedule regular exercise, eat a balanced diet, and prioritize sleep. Incorporate mindfulness practices like meditation or journaling to help manage stress and maintain focus. Remember, your health is your most valuable asset.

9. Practice Generosity: Look for ways to give back to your community, whether through charitable donations, volunteering, or mentoring others. Generosity not only benefits those around you but also adds meaning and fulfillment to your life.

10. Stay Persistent: Above all, commit to persistence. The road to financial success will have its ups and downs, but by staying focused, positive, and resilient, you will eventually achieve your goals. Remember that progress takes time, and small, consistent efforts will compound over time to create significant results.

Embracing Consistency, Self-Belief, and Growth

As you begin to incorporate these habits into your life, remember that consistency is key. It's not about making radical changes overnight, but rather about committing to small, manageable actions that you can sustain over time. Success is a journey, and those who stay the course, adapt to challenges, and continuously grow are the ones who ultimately reach their goals.

Self-belief is equally important. Millionaires have confidence in their ability to overcome obstacles, learn from failures, and achieve their dreams. By cultivating a strong sense of self-belief and maintaining a growth mindset, you can stay motivated and resilient in the face of challenges.

Finally, embrace the idea of continuous growth. Financial success is not a destination, but an ongoing process of learning, improving, and evolving. As you continue to grow, both personally and professionally, you will unlock new opportunities and reach levels of success you once thought were out of reach.

* 9 7 9 8 3 3 0 5 9 5 3 5 8 *